You Will Find a Way

You Will Find a Way

The Inner Spirit of Golf

Corbin L. Cherry

HGG Publishers
MILL VALLEY, CALIFORNIA

First printing 2003

ISBN 0-9721497-1-6
LCCN 2002108910

ATTENTION CORPORATIONS, UNIVERSITIES, COLLEGES, AND PROFES-SIONAL ORGANIZATIONS: Quantity discounts are available on bulk purchases of this book for educational, gift purposes, or as premiums for increasing magazine subscriptions or renewals. Special books or book excerpts can also be created to fit specific needs. For information, please contact HGG Publishers, 245 Morningsun Ave., Mill Valley, CA 94941; (415) 388-8221.

I want to dedicate this book to all of those people I play golf with voluntarily.
They make this game what it truly needs to be and that is fun. I also dedicate it to my Lord and my Links.

"Excellence in golf, as in life, is never an accident; it is the result of high intention, sincere effort, intelligent direction, skilled execution and the vision to see obstacles as opportunities.... Golf is deceptively simple and endlessly complicated. It satisfies the soul and frustrates the intellect. It is at the same time rewarding and maddening. It is without a doubt the greatest game mankind has ever invented."

—ARNOLD PALMER

— TABLE OF CONTENTS —

In the Garden

I feel privileged to be able to create this book relative to golf and other dimensions and to share the wonderful feelings I have for this game and the people, places, and things to which this game has granted me access. In these pages I hope to share some true stories and experiences. I hope to answer some questions that might arise in a golfer's mind and pose still some other questions dealing with this great game and man's (and woman's) more-than-mundane approach to the philosophical nature of this game.

Golf is a wonderful game that has touched many people. In this book I will try to show how golf can reach both the divine and human natures of those who choose to participate in it. I will also try to search the depths of some of the lives of those who have endeavored to and indeed have truly and deeply communed with golf. I want to pass along to any who might read these words, just what this game has given to me and what it has come to mean to me in the past three decades. I must say that these thoughts are mine and mine alone. I say this because I can only speak for myself, and that I intend to do at this time and in these pages. Yes, these thoughts are mine, but they can be attested to by many people other than myself, and I am willing to share them with any who desire to take the time to ask about them and to listen to them.

I want to say up front that I never won any major golf tournaments, yet I have walked in "the Garden" and I have tasted the fruit. I am willing to wager it tastes no better to anyone else, anywhere in the entire world, than it does to me. I say this, not to boast, but rather to make it clear I am writing this book because of how I feel about this great game. I believe my feelings about the game of golf run deeper than most people will ever be able to realize in their own golf lives. That does not make me better than they are, just more fortunate.

As a young boy I learned an important lesson: It is necessary to have some sort of a relationship with God. Please do not put this book down, because it is not going to be a book about sermons and religion. Instead, I hope it will only be what you need for it to be or what you want it to be. For me, through all of these years, having God in my life has not only granted me peace, but it has centered my life so peace can happen in all phases of my life—including golf.

I remember high school and college football and baseball coaches praying before a game and asking God for victory in that particular contest. Asking God for victory was never the right approach for me. I guess I figured He had a great deal of other things to do that seemed far more important than a mere football game. On the other hand, I have asked God to use me in certain situations and to give me strength to be a better example, or an example period. Still I have never asked God to use His considerable talents to help me to kick a field goal to win a game, or to hit a home run to that same end, or even to shoot 68 on the golf course to win a golf tournament.

I have participated in many sports in my life. At some of them I was fairly good, while at others I was not so talented. None of those sports has ever granted me the same level of peace I have found from playing golf. It may sound silly or even strange, but I have had spiritual feelings because of a specific time and a special golf course on which I was playing. Those times have made me happy to be part of a beautiful world and more aware of where I am in the survival chain.

There have been many times when just smelling the aroma of a flowering bush, like a honeysuckle, or seeing cherry blossoms and azaleas in bloom that a sense of spirituality was so significant inside of me. It was as real and as prominent as the smells and sights that were mine right there in those days and they were there just for the taking. I have felt that way many times in my golf life and as you read these lines, if you have not witnessed these special feelings in your life, you have been deprived of far more than you can ever imagine. You have missed a significant part of the greatest of games. I call this area in my relationship with golf *the part of the heart.*

The following was written many years ago, but it certainly has relevance to the game of life and the game of golf. I am sure the author never played a round of golf in his whole life, yet he truly understood what it takes to play this game and to live through the game of life.

> *Let nothing disturb you,*
> *Let nothing frighten you,*
> *All things are passing,*
> *God alone is changeless,*
> *Patient endurance attains all things.*

The meaning behind these words works for me as a pattern in my walk through life and my relationship with the game of golf. I know many people who have been able to see the reality of these thoughts in their relationship to their golf game and also in their relationship to the game of life, which we are all trying to play every day, I hope. Indeed patient endurance can allow the attainment of a great number of objectives in life and golf.

Golf is so different from most other sports, especially team sports. In the game of golf, for the most part, you stand alone against 6,850 yards of beautiful green grass, some of it longer than we might like it to be, water hazards, sand traps, the wind, the rain, many well-hidden obstacles, as well as trees of every size and species, and of course 18 sometimes elusive holes. The most notable opponent we face every time we play is ourselves. When we play this game honorably, most of the time our mind is our foremost opponent. It can cause good things and bad things to happen in our personal lives as well as in our game.

For me, the way I have to approach this game is in a scientific manner with what I like to call emotional fallout. What that specifically means for me is that I need to be diligent in my approach to learning the game of golf; then I need to love what I might have learned. In trying to learn the right way to play the game one needs to understand the need for practicing and practicing the right things, the correct way.

This premise shall be repeated time and time again in the pages ahead. Along with this is the fact that the proper thoughts and feelings can be a sort of salvation as we wander into places that are filled with self-imposed demons, like doubt, indecision, greed, and often feeling as if there is no hope whatsoever for improvement in our golf game. One of the worst and most formidable of all demons we might face in this game of golf is the lack of confidence. To me that sounds a great deal like the situations many people face in their everyday lives. So we are already back to our minds.

We must endeavor to play this game for the right reasons such as joy and happiness. It is in our best interest to try to limit the amount of frustration we feel because of this game to a minimum level. This game, with all of its beauty and wonderment, can easily become a game of fury and pain. It, above all else, should be a game of enjoyment and positiveness. Watch the big-name pros on all three of the pro golf tours when they are having a bad day or a bad tournament. The expression on their faces would make you think they hate this game, they hate the golf courses on which they are playing, they hate their golf clubs, and they indeed hate their caddies. Yet the truth of the matter is that they love the game of golf and all of its positive components, even though it often drives them into a deep valley of doubt. That is obvious because they keep coming back for one more dose of this thing we call golf. These feelings are merely part of a love-hate relationship with the game of golf that they have built through the years,. That love-hate relationship goes right down the golf success ladder to where all of us who play this game find ourselves.

As we take this journey through these upcoming pages, let us never put aside the reality that golf is only a game and one that is to be enjoyed and not agonized over. Having said this I realize that is easier said than done. I have a friend from England, whom I met while snow skiing many years ago. Whenever we got together in the wintertime for skiing, like all golfers we talked a great deal about golf. We talked about equipment and golf courses we have played and things that golfers like to discuss. Yet because of logistics we were never able to actually play a round of golf together. After many years and many golf stories, he was on a trip to California and he decided to come to visit me for two days while his wife went to visit her relatives in another part of the state. We finally got to play golf together and I felt really bad for him, because, according to him, he played the worst 2 rounds of golf in his entire golf life. Of course everything has to be taken into account as to its relativity anyway.

Everything that could happen to him, happened to him. He hit balls right and left, in hazards and out of bounds. He was frustrated and down, to say the least. That is just one of the things that this game can do to us. After the second day of such mentally depleting golf for him we went to the San Francisco Airport to pick up his wife, who was flying in from Los Angeles. He sat in the backseat and she sat in the front seat, being her usually wonderful and peppy self. She turned and looked at him, in his remorseful and solemn state and asked, "What is wrong dear?"

He replied to her inquiry in a morose manner. "Oh, love, I played two of the worst rounds of golf in the past couple of days I could ever imagine." Then he heard the most crushing and yet most truthful words ever bestowed upon him or anyone else who is a serious golfer and feeling downhearted about their game and trapped in that valley of darkness that golf can drag us into. "Well you know, Honey, it is only a game." He was not consoled.

These words, though they are so often killers in our already time of pain, are the truest of all words relative to this great game and we must never forget their importance. For this game is only a game, always and foremost. In our lives recreation is important. It can change our lives forever and we need to always remember that fact. Henry Ward Beecher said it best: "There can be no high civilization where there is not ample leisure." We do need games in our lives and golf is indeed a game that can really and truly be enjoyed if we take it in the proper dosage.

The game of golf does bring us both high and low emotional swings, but the highs are more numerous and of far more importance than the lows. We need to concentrate on the victories and let the losses go away like a bad dream. I believe the lows can actually be highs at some point, because of who we are with, where we are, and who we are. David Forgan wrote the following and I want to share this with each person who reads this book because it is an accurate description of the game we call golf. "Golf is a science, the study of a lifetime, in which you may exhaust yourself but never your subject. It is a contest, a duel or a melee, calling for courage, skill, strategy and self control. It is a test of temper, a trial of honor, a revealer of character. It affords the chance to play the man and act the gentleman. It means going into God's out-of-doors, getting close to nature, fresh air, exercise, a sweeping away of the mental cobwebs and genuine re-creation of the tired tissues. It is a sure cure for care, an antidote to worry. It includes companionship with friends, social intercourse, opportunities for courtesy, kindliness, and generosity to an opponent. It promotes not only physical health, but moral force."

That is a fair synopsis of the game of golf. Once we understand that golf is not just a day, but it is a lifetime, then we can understand it as the relationship that it can be or already is. It is indeed akin to a relationship we might find in philosophy, religion, and/or spirituality. Still it is only a game. If we understand those elements therein mentioned then we can truly start to understand this great and grand game.

So let us get started and talk about golf and its depths. This can also be a marvelous voyage into life itself, as we try to understand a little more about the game of golf and the game of life. Both can be of great value to us, young and old alike. Come and go with me into "the Garden"…

CHAPTER ONE

The Early Days

Many, many years ago—almost too many now to remember, yet only a fool would be able to forget—a young man of twenty-one years in High Point, North Carolina, walked into a pawnshop for the first time in his life. Though it was also the last time up to this point, now all these years later his life was forever changed. Changed, yes, but darted with so many moments of joy than is possibly allowable in the lives of a hundred people, let alone the life of just that one young man.

There in that place jam-packed with so many different items, from every corner of the world, on a shelf just above the cash register was something strange to his eyes, but at the same time interesting and alluring. There on the shelf was something that many people who play golf today probably have never even seen. A starter set of golf clubs, a 1 wood, a 3 wood and 4 irons, a 3, a 5, a 7 and a 9, plus a putter. Today in our world of merchandise sale extravaganzas there are few starter sets of golf clubs still out there on the market. Normally when someone buys a set of golf clubs today they get the whole package, whether they want it or not. There are normally 3 woods, the 2 or 3 iron, all the way through the pitching wedge, whether the sets are cheap or not so cheap. That is usually the makeup of a full set of golf clubs. Most of the time a set of golf clubs is not so cheap.

When the young man saw these clubs in their little green golf bag, a light came on, and he said to his friend K. D., "This might be fun." This turned out to be an understatement of major magnitude and monumental proportion. For 55 dollars he got the seven golf clubs, three brand new Capri golf balls, the small green golf bag (equal to the task of carrying the aforementioned golf clubs), and an amazing odyssey began.

The first day of golf in that young man's life, which I am sure you have realized by now was yours truly, began with the paying of my first green fee of five dollars (many things have certainly changed through the years) and a walk to the 1st tee with my friend K. D. (who was not a first-timer as I was).

Standing there on the 1st tee—and I mean the first tee in my entire golf life—I had no idea what was out there ahead of me. I had no inkling of what was in store for me on that day, let alone all of the days, years, and decades that lay ahead out there in the future. At that point those times ahead were not important to me. The whole concept of the game was so new to me that I did not even know how to hold the golf club. Because I was a college student, I was quickly able to figure out which end of the club to grip, but from there on I was more or less in the dark. More, I think.

So with no practice, something that I would never think of doing today, I attempted to hit the golf ball off of the 1st tee. I tried hitting the ball again and again and finally I did hit it. As it exploded off of the club face, (of course I am exaggerating just a little) it flew a tad to the right. In my golf life now, that much to the right would be a great deal to the right, but then it was only a bit to the right. Yes, just a tad. Yet I did find it, there it was, a Capri 1. For a moment I was startled, for as I looked around upon approaching my ball there were golf balls everywhere. I remember thinking "this is fun" and knowing full well that I would never have to buy another golf ball for the rest of my life and all of this on my maiden day of golf. So I began picking up the balls by the handfuls and as I was putting them in my new green bag, I was totally unaware of the large and angry man standing far away, jumping up and down and screaming in my direction. How was I to know what a shag ball was and for that matter, what a driving range was? I had never practiced before.

With some disappointment I removed the golf balls from my new green golf bag (I guess I got them all out of there), waved an apology to the big man for whatever I had done to enrage him, and proceeded to hit my second shot. (I may have been out of bounds on my first shot, but I, of course, did not even know what out of bounds was on that premiere day. I have learned since.) I mean it was my first day at playing or rather attempting to play this great game. Once we were out of ear-shot of where the large man was hitting those golf balls, K. D. explained to me that I had hit my ball into a practice area, then I understood the man's anger. I would see that part of golf again, the anger I mean. I shot 116 for my first 18 holes of golf, I guess I counted them all.

About three days later, or so, I was playing my second round of golf, at the same golf course there in High Point and again with my friend K. D. With a number of holes behind us, a great many shots later, and probably a few lost golf balls also, we reached the 12th hole. My tee shot on the 12th hole went to the right again, as so many of my shots had a way of doing in those early years, and it rolled down a steep slope into a small patch of woods. When I went down the hill into the trees to search for my errant ball I found a golf ball, but it was not mine. Instead of a Capri 1, it was a Tit-lest 1 and as I read the name on the ball I found it strange that someone would give that name to a golf ball. I had to laugh to myself thinking some really dumb person would manufacture a golf ball and name it after a part of the female anatomy. (Probably an off brand, I thought to myself, and they probably never sell many of them.)

About that time I came upon a middle-aged man and woman in the woods, also searching for a ball, I guess. The forty-ish woman asked if I had by chance found a golf ball and I proudly proclaimed, "Yes, ma'am it is a Tit-lest." She smiled and asked if it had a one on it and I said yes and assuming that it was hers, I proudly gave it to her. She smiled and asked if golf was a new game for me. I indicated that it was, probably grinned, and wondered just how she knew that because she had not seen my golf swing. If she had seen me take a swipe at the golf ball it would have most likely been a dead giveaway.

K. D. came running over to me after the couple walked away and informed me that the golf ball that I found was a Titlest and not a Tit-lest. Then I realized that the woman had not seen my swing and I fully understood just how she knew that I was new at this sport. I felt somewhat embarrassed, maybe one of the few times in my golf life to this date, not because of any great skill on my part, but rather because golf has always been and seemed to me to be too special to feel or be embarrassed about.

I guess embarrassment is a stepchild of either disappointment or anger. Those two elements have fortunately been absent most of my golf life. The game of golf has brought me joy, love, and peace and I guess those elements have been the children of my relationship with golf through the years. From those first two days of golf with K. D. I was going to learn about many things relative to golf, and frustration was one of those elements.

As I learned more about the game of golf and the people who love it and play it with heated, deep passion and desire, and as I watched people with a great amount of skill or limited skills, as those skills related to golf and how both approach this game, I came to know a little something about frustration and a great deal about desire and passion. Fortunately for me the desire and passion for this game grew and the frustration ebbed and flowed silently away and out of my golf life, for the most part.

The years between that first 116 and the time of the 80s (scores not the years) seemed to pass as if they were some sort of a blur. There were many rounds of golf, for just about every chance I had to play, I did so. There were thousands of practice shots and I am sure some of them were correct practice shots and some were not. There were few times or days of frustration as they related to golf and a great many times of saying, "I love this game."

There was even one night in Atlanta, when I went to a driving range and hit more than 400 golf balls in a short span of time. The next morning found me in my bed and unable to get out of it because I had such extreme pain in my lower back. I learned a valuable lesson from that experience and that was that we—and in this particular case, me—should not swing a golf club at a golf ball as hard as I did on that driving range. It was only one lesson of so many that I was going to learn before I realized that if I do not approach this game correctly that golf will always win, and I will be left in the bed or somewhere else with a bad back and a confused mind.

I am one of the fortunate few who loves what he does as a profession and what he has as an avocation. I often think long and hard about how the road through both of those worlds has been paved with so much laughter, joy, and fulfillment that it is truly almost unbelievable. I say almost because I know, from personal experience, that it does, can, and has happened.

On one occasion in my early years of golf, a friend of mine and I were playing golf on one of the golf courses where we had played many times before. On that particular day my friend hit his tee shot a bit to the right and into a lake just adjacent to the fairway on the 6th hole. As we were fishing around for his golf ball, in that dark and grimy-looking water, we happened to find several other golf balls in good condition. Then we came up with a very—I would say *smart* plan, but that might not be the most accurate way to describe this particular plan. We decided to come back later in the dead of night and go into the lake and see just how many golf balls we could really find in there.

Later that night, around 9:30 or so, with flashlights and garbage bags in hand, we worked our way from the road to the 6th hole, in search of golf ball treasures. We remarked that the golf course, and particularly the lake, looked quite different in the darkness than it had those hours earlier, in the daylight. We never thought about the snakes, leeches, or other various and sundry denizens of the deep, which could have been lurking around there in that murky and dark water. Would I do that now? I think not! Still with all of that intelligence, which we showed in our adventure into the lake, the mission was quite a success. We recovered over 400 golf balls, some good and some not so good, but in the dark it was truly hard to tell the difference, Tit-lest and all. We just knew we would never have to buy another golf ball for the rest of our lives. I had thought that same thought earlier in my golf life. I was wrong both times.

We took the trash bags filled with golf balls back to the house where my wife and I lived at the time and we emptied them all in the bathtub. What a great find, what a haul, boy what a mess! What a basic misunderstanding with my wife. It wasn't so much a misunderstanding on my part as it was on hers. You see I knew what I was doing and she did not know what I was doing because she kept asking me over and over again, "Corbin, what are you planning on doing with all of those golf balls in the bathtub?" I knew that they were there so I could wash the mud off of them, but I guess she did not understand that. It seemed rather simple to me.

I love this game and I have from the start. K. D. wherever you are on this day, I love you for getting me started on this incredible journey into my life of golf and into a love for this great game.

> *With little knowledge and many dreams,*
> *Humanity seeks to understand deeper and better*
> *All of the obstinate forces that surround and*
> *   crowd in around him*
> *And cause him pain and yet give him great joy.*

— CHAPTER TWO —

Peace Comes With Knowledge

There have been many books written, by many different people, expounding all of the levels and ramifications of all of the levels of this great game. At least all of those levels that we, as humans, know about, care about, and understand. Yet few truly have ventured into the spiritual side of this game that so many people love. I, in no way mean to infer or imply that golf replaces God in the universe for me. Yet for some, and even many, elements like God, love, and so many other beautiful issues of life are either clouded or are just outright forgotten, because of humanity's fascination with the game of golf.

This is not a new theory, but it is a reality. In our lives we can all recall situations from our friendship circles where golf became a problem, and not just a game, for someone whom we knew or know. I have known people who actually lost their families because of their relationship with golf. It can be much the same as a person who has a drug, drinking, or gambling problem. If any one of us is guilty of this approach to the game of golf then we need to rethink and reevaluate our concept of the game and our approach to it. If we spend too much time doing any one thing and no time or little time doing the other things in our lives, then it seems that the scales are out of balance. If we approach golf, or anything else for that matter, in that fashion there is something wrong with our perspective.

However I would like to draw my reasoning on this subject of fascination from a different plane, another level where all of the beautiful things in life are brought into a special focus by one's love for something special such as walking, biking, and yes even playing golf. This I might add is or at least can be the purest kind of love and it has oh so many different tentacles of emotion. If you have ever walked alone on a late autumn afternoon, with your golf bag on your shoulder, observing the leaves, so vivid in their colors, as the sun is slowly finishing that day's trek across the sky, you know something of what makes these emotions come alive.

As I walk, I think about my views on life, the numerous blessings that I am so fortunate to have, my feelings about spiritual certainties and those concepts that are less than certainties. I think about my family, my friends, and the memories of years in this great sport, with victories for which I have no trophies to show, save a thousand smiles. When I recall a chip shot—which by luck or otherwise went into the hole—or a long putt destined for the cup, or better yet a special time spent with friends and the utopian elements that such a time can provide, I also think about what a wonderful thing it is to have this peace in my life, when all around me there are so many others who have no peace in theirs, though they should.

Then I think about what could add more meaning and pleasure to this picture. Oh I guess maybe I could win the lottery and if so what would I do with the money? I have to smile when I think that if I ever did win that lottery, it would only allow me more time to do all of these same things and be with all of these same people, even more than I am now, and therefore have all of these good thoughts time and time again. Still in the final analysis it all comes down to one thing and that is being at peace with myself and with all of the elements around me, human and otherwise.

That is one of the good things that golf can grant us if we are open to have that place of peace in our lives. In this day of fast electric and gas golf carts it is truly harder to find that peace, but be not dismayed for it is still out there waiting for all of us. We just have to try a little harder to find it, but it is worth the search. I remember standing in the fairway on the 1st hole of the Plantation Course at the Kapalua Golf Club, on the Island of Maui, a few years ago, waiting to hit my second shot and watching the whales so joyfully playing in the Pacific Ocean. I will tell you, peace was not far away from my mind and heart on that day. It is there for us if we want it and endeavor to find it.

The key is whether we want that emotion in our golf life or not. It is important to understand that we do not have to be on the Island of Maui to find that special time for ourselves. Some people never even think about peaceful things when they play golf because they are not prone to think about peace as it relates to golf or anything else, just playing the game. Still there are others who do think about it because they have been into that "Garden" and they are happy they have found a special peace and place, through and in this game.

That is what golf allows us in this context. If we want it, it can be found, but many people go out every week and play this game and never even think about all of the joy and serenity this game can offer them. I feel bad for those people who are just too busy to enjoy what this wonderful game is really and truly all about. I have quite often played golf with people who always wear their beepers or pagers on their belts when they play. As a result they are constantly on their cellular telephones with their brokers, their wives, their friends, or they are talking to the office about things that are probably important. The point I am making here is that in doing all of these outside things, as important or not as they may be, they are missing out on the truest of elements of this special place, this special hour, and this special walk in time. This time on the golf course should be used in contemplation of what lies ahead in these hours that can truly be magic.

We need to think about things like, how far is it to the pin? Is the pin in the front, the middle, or the back of the green? Is there any wind and if there is wind will it affect the flight of my shot? Is it blowing from the left or from the right? Is the shot uphill or downhill and do I need to fade the shot, hit it straight, or try to draw it? Will the green be soft or hard? What is my club choice? All of these things consume time and brain function and they are important in our attempting to conquer the golf course on which we are playing, and they are extremely valuable elements in the total golf experience. To not think about and feel those elements as we play this game is to miss a great deal of the real positive parts of the experience of golf.

The pager and cellular phone can rob us of those elements if we allow that to happen. The truth of the matter is that many people play golf to just get away from things around them and by still dealing with all of the issues they sought to elude, by way of the electronic medium at their disposal, they fail to get away at all. Different people play golf for many different reasons and some of those people do not want peace in their days or in their lives and that is all right for them. Still for those of us who love this game for the peacefulness it allows us, there are few places better to be, if any…

There have been few times in my life when I have carried a pager with me while I was playing golf, but that was out of sheer necessity because of work. I am sure that most people who carry pagers with them feel the same way. I only mention this because on those occasions when I was paged while playing golf I played my worst golf of the day following those interruptions. I bring this up here because we cannot always dodge our other-than-golf responsibilities, but many times we are forced mentally to think more about the other things than we do about our golf game, when in reality we could ethically forget about those outside-of-the-golf-realm things, at least for a while. When the beeper goes off and you do not answer the page, you are automatically drawn into wondering and worrying if there are things you need to take care of. If you do decide to answer the page your mind tries to shake the call, to get back to the business at hand, which is the golf course; but, try as we may, our humanity usually will not allow that to happen. Most of the time we cannot dodge or forget the issues surrounding the page. That is a human shortcoming called responsibility or guilt, or maybe both. So we find ourselves caught between a rock and a hard place and most likely not able to concentrate like we should on the rest of the holes left to play in our round. To play at our best we have to be able to concentrate and to be at peace.

In my early years as a golfer—and I use that term golfer loosely relative to my younger years—I went through a time when I just had to get out and play golf every spare moment that I could find. I would get up at five o'clock in the morning to try and play 9 holes of golf before I went to a class or to a meeting, or instead of either.

I would rush to the golf course in the afternoon after work or instead of work, to play as many holes as I could get in before it got to be so dark that I could not even see the golf ball after it was hit or even before it was hit, on some occasions. There were days when I played 36 holes many afternoons and upon reaching the final hole all I could see were the lights from the swimming pool, which was adjacent to the 18th hole at that particular golf course. I knew that the 18th green was just to the right side of the swimming pool so that was where I endeavored to hit my shot. So I hit shots at the shadows, where the green used to be before it got to be so dark that I could not see it. I am sure that some of the golf balls I was never able to find, must have found their way into that swimming hole on those wonderful, calm, and dark evenings.

I cannot count or even remember all of the times I have played 54 holes of golf in a given day, but I do remember the 72-hole marathons in which I played, yes and in one day. We played fast and we played without thinking just because we loved the game and we were addicted to it. The funny thing in all of this is that in those years I thought I did love the game of golf and in a strange and macabre kind of way I truly did, yet it was different then than it has become in recent years. For one thing I have learned more about the game of golf and the joy and peace it can give to those of us fortunate enough to approach it from that much softer side and place. In those early days the reverence, yes the true reverence for the game of golf was missing, not out of intent but rather because of the lack of knowledge. It was go out and hit the ball and get the mission accomplished and that was that.

Today it seems there is a great deal more to the game of golf for me than awaking at the break of dawn and getting to the golf course just to play in a hurry, as if to be finished with it. I now want to practice each day before I play. I do not want to be rushed and above all I want to have a good time when I finally get around to playing a particular round of golf. Oh yes I am still on a quest, but the quest seems different than it was before and that is merely because it seems that I have a plan, not just for golf, but also for the relationship that I have with golf, to make it better and better, year after year. That quest is a desire I have to play new places and more times with favorite familiar faces. There is a great difference now than in those early days and years. Be well assured that the intensity is still there, but it some-how has been treated with knowledge and tempered with some level of maturity.

I still play golf most every chance that I get, but it is so de-lightfully different. I still play 36 holes on many days, but that too has changed. I do not like to play in the rain and unless I am playing in a tournament I will surely forego the chance and plea-sure to play a round of golf in that kind of weather and under those adverse conditions. In those years before I would have considered myself to be a wimp for not venturing out into what I now consider to be awful conditions, but that has changed, as have my feelings about this game.

Two years ago I played a round of golf in Richmond, Vir-ginia, in late April and it was so cold I that I could not unzip my pants to go to the restroom. I once played a round of golf in the dead of winter on ground that was frozen solid and the lake on the golf course was frozen all the way across. I remember hitting a golf ball across the lake and listening to the pinging sound coming from the ice every time the ball hit it. That was prob-ably the longest drive of my life, to that point and because I will not be out there anymore on an ice-covered lake to play golf, it will no doubt be my longest drive ever. No more. I will no longer crawl into those dirty lakes searching for golf balls, though the thoughts aggressively still cross my mind on certain occasions.

Still I am motivated by the greatest game in the world, but I no longer have to play it. I now want to play and play as often as I possibly can and that alone has granted me a great deal of peace in my life and with my golf. Most people do not understand this level of emotion in their relationship with golf, merely because they have not been introduced to that mental level of this game by someone else's example or they have not yet reached that level of understanding for themselves. Being on this emotional level with golf does not make me better than anyone else who is out there, just more fortunate.

Jack Nicklaus once said that when he was young and he first started playing golf, it was because he liked the sport and the feelings he received from it. He then said that he continued to play golf for all of these years, in which he has electrified millions of people all over the world with his brilliant play, because he fell in love with the game. I watched him walk down the 18th fairway at Pebble Beach, playing in the 2000 U.S. Open with tears just streaming from his eyes. He was thinking that possibly that stroll might be his final one in a U.S. Open. Was he feeling love for the game of golf? You can safely bet that he was. That says it all. One's relationship with golf can grow from an immature one to a full-blown mature feeling relationship through years of doing something that is so elusive and yet fulfilling. A relationship that can make us feel good and can show us some definite peace of mind and heart. Those are the same elements on which other sound relationships in our lives are built like relationships with our spouses, our children, and yes even with God. Many people, myself included, can find emotional and spiritual peace in this game we love. For me, that is one of the reasons I feel a special harmony between my God and my golf.

Some years ago, on a cold and blustery day, on a trip to the north of Scotland I was feeling a bit alone because of certain emotional events in my life at that time. I stopped at a local golf course on the western coast of that golfdom. I paid my green fee and put my golf bag on my shoulder and proceeded to play a round of golf on that particular golf course. I played all right I guess, but it was wonderful. The truth was that how I played mattered little to me at that point. I was out there and not a soul was to be seen except those passengers passing by on the infrequent comings and goings of the commuter trains in that part of the world. The skies were dark, as if there was a storm pending, but the only storm was the one inside of me as I started that walk. There were some negative thoughts and feelings running through my head, but it was then that I remembered all of the many blessings in my life and all of the wonderful people I was fortunate enough to call my family and my friends. In some cases they are the same. That moment drew me closer to the realization that God has always taken good care of me through the years. I knew down deep inside of myself that fact would not change. I guess in that three-hour-or-so walk I felt as if my burdens were all lifted and I was going to be all right. When I finally arrived back at my car, my heart was less heavy and as I looked back at that old golf course and at the still dark, late evening sky, there was a prayerful moment of thanksgiving, for both my Lord and my links.

There is peace here in this wonderful game, but we have to approach it in the correct fashion to find it for ourselves.

> *Seeking peace in golf is quite often a journey with absolutely no end,*
> *A road filled with land mines and holes so deep we can be therein lost forever.*
> *Yet if we are fortunate enough to find that elusive path to peace,*
> *We just might be indeed one of the most fortunate few.*

— CHAPTER THREE —

Being at the Masters

In those early years of trying to learn about this game and playing it as much as possible, I was also at the seminary at Emory University in Atlanta, Georgia. It was there I awoke in the early hours of many mornings, to try and get some golf in before—or as I stated previously, even instead of—going to class. To say the least I was infatuated with this game. A friend of mine approached me one day and asked if I had ever thought about working during the Masters Week in Augusta as a gallery guard. I, of course had no knowledge about what this job entailed, but I inquired anyway. To my surprise I was accepted by the Pinkerton Detective Agency as a gallery guard, to work there at the Augusta National Golf Club, for the entire week of that great golf tournament. I had no idea what was in store for me in that first week and the years which fortunately followed it. That place was and is a magic spot in so many ways and especially during that special week of the year.

The first year that I worked there at the Masters, as one might expect, I was totally awestruck by just walking around the grounds and seeing not only all of the greatest players of that time, from all over the world, but by the sheer beauty of that piece of property. I was assigned as a gallery guard and it was truly both a mind-boggling and thrilling experience.

My job was to walk inside of the ropes with the players to whom I was assigned and clear paths for them when they reached the areas where the galleries were all jammed together, waiting to watch the next shots from each of their golf heroes. I saw not only great golf shots, but I got to walk side by side with the likes of Arnold Palmer (they were truly the days of Arnie's Army). I watched Jack Nicklaus begin his assault on the golf world. Sam Snead was still playing. As was Ben Hogan and Billy Casper. I watched Tony Lema almost win there and I witnessed his press conference and television interview when he gave an amazing amount of praise to God for his good fortune. Yes, that is correct, the party boy himself, Champagne Tony Lema on that day was in God's corner.

Many others like George Baer, Ed Furgol, Gene Sarazen, Gene Littler, Bob Rosburg, and the Hebert Brothers were all there. All of the great names in golf were hitting wonderful shots and some not so wonderful shots. Yet it was, for a novice like me, a world away from where I thought I would ever be. On one occasion I was privileged to be introduced to the great Bobby Jones, but I did not know much about him at that time or his impact on golf until some years later. He had a relationship with his golf game, in his day, which was monumental and that is putting it mildly. As I watched him sitting there in his wheelchair next to the teebox on hole number 10, it was difficult to imagine his overpowering golf game.

Watching those men play that great golf course and observing their expertise was, as I said earlier, mind-boggling. That event was such an experience for me I went there on that special week for five straight years. I heard wonderful stories and I saw history happen. I saw tempers flare and listened to obscenities paint the air blue. I watched a grown man throw his clubs, bag and all, into the lake that guards the 15th green and turn to his caddie, who must have believed that he might be the next to go into the water, and merely say, "I will see you at the car." I then watched him walk toward the clubhouse, stop, and snap his fingers on remembering that the keys to his car were in that wet golf bag. He walked back to the water's edge, waded into the lake, and retrieved his golf bag, took the keys out of the bag and returned it to the darkness of the lake. Some people laughed and seemed amused, but I found that whole affair rather unsettling for me, even in those early days of my golf.

I also witnessed some other absurd and bizarre behavior on the part of some of those players and I was to find out later that absurd behavior is not reserved for the elite in this game, or for the nonelite. We are all capable of exhibiting that kind of attitude. Let me just mention one event to illustrate how absurd this whole game of golf can get, if we allow our minds to function in that canal. I was assigned on this particular day to a certain group of players. We were on the 14th hole. One of the players— and if I did mention his name, it would be a familiar name to most golfers who have some golf years under their belts—while he was squatting down behind his ball and trying to read the line of the putt that was facing him, he hesitated and looked right straight at me. At first I thought I had done something to distract him. He walked over to me and asked me to walk to the far side of the adjoining fairway and instruct about 300 or so people walking along that fairway to stop walking so he could putt and not be distracted.

I thought to myself, "This guy is crazy." Those people were nearly two football fields away. I learned a valuable lesson from that, which was that this game, as great as it is, does promote a great deal of mental unrest, tension, and disorder. That has been proven over and over again as I have matured in the mental aspects of golf.

I saved a place in these musings for some stories about the Masters, because they were definitely defining moments for me, as far as my maturing into learning about golf was concerned, but also because along with many special things that happened there, one specific event occurred that changed lives forever, one of which was mine. It was my second year of working there in Augusta. I had been sent out late on that Sunday morning with two players, both of whom were in contention for the Green Jacket. Most who read this may or may not know that the Green Jacket is awarded each year to the winner of the Masters Golf Championship. My assigned player was starting that fourth and final round only two shots behind the leader. On the 2nd hole, the player to whom I was assigned hooked his tee shot off of the tee and into the woods on the left side of the fairway. From the moment he left the teebox, his head was down and shaking and he was angrily talking to himself. He never looked up all the way to where his ball had entered the woods. When we got to his ball ("we" because it was the player, his caddie, an official, and me), it had come to rest in a small stream of water and only about one-third of the ball was protruding out of the water. He started swearing and using God's name in vane and as he did I turned away. He saw me turn away and asked me, "What did you say?" He was angry.

I just shook my head and moved still further away from him, because we had been instructed to never confront or talk to any of the players unless they approached us first. We had further been told to stay out of the players way, at all cost. Still he persisted and asked me yet again just what I had said. I answered his question by saying merely, that I had said nothing at all, which by the way was the truth.

He then said to me in a stern manner, "You say it to me right now face to face or you walk off of this golf course this minute." I was not looking at a pretty sight. Yet I replied by saying, "Your ball went left because you hit it left and it ended up in this stream because you hit it there. That was not God's fault, but yours. It seemed to me that you rolled your hands over too much." I did not know much about hands at that point in my golf life, but still it seemed to make sense to me.

He looked at me as if he wanted to kill me and I am sure, to this day, that he probably did, but he never said a word to me. He reached into his golf bag and retrieved his rain pants and then sled aggressively into them. I am sure that he put them on to keep from getting his bright purple pants wet and/or muddy. He took a 2 iron out of his caddie's hand, stepped into the small stream of water and with a beautiful golf swing, he not only hit the ball out of the water, but he hit one of the greatest golf shots I have ever seen in my entire life, to this day. He went on to make a birdie on that hole and better yet on that beautiful Sunday afternoon in Augusta, Georgia, he went on to win his first and only Masters title. After our exchange, prior to that magnificent shot, he never spoke another word to me all the way around the golf course, but I saw him glance in my direction on several occasions. My IQ is not 250, but I did know to keep my distance from him for the rest of that round.

In those years when a gallery guard was fortunate enough to be with a winner of the Masters, it was his job to stay with the player until all of the ceremonies were finished and the player exited the golf course. During the ceremony when he was being presented his official Green Jacket, I was still keeping my distance from him. I ventured closer to get a better look at him and it was then that he motioned for me to come to where he was standing. He had his victory check in his hand and he reached out and pulled me closer to his side. When I got up next to him, he showed me the check and he said, "Do you see this?"

I nodded my head in the affirmative. "If I ever use God's name in vain again I will give you half of it." I tried to remember just how much the check was for, but I could not for the life of me recall the amount because I was caught up in that special moment and the check really did not seem to matter much at all. What mattered most in my mind and heart was that God had won. I was truly shocked by what had happened. I knew he was in the midst of an emotional high brought about by his great victory. I shook his hand, smiled, congratulated him, and slid back into the crowd of well-wishers and officials.

I could stop the story here and it would be a nice one and that would be that, but it would be simply incomplete. I watched this Masters Champion's career though the years go up and down, as most of the careers do in that business. The years passed, 23 to be exact, and I was playing in a Pro-Am tournament at the Silverado Golf Club, a few miles north of San Francisco. I was standing on the practice range preparing to hit some warm-up shots before my time came to tee off. I looked up and down the range, as I was warming up, to see just who was hitting golf shots and there he was. He was a little heavier, a little grayer, but the swing was still there and I joyfully recalled that day, so many years before and so far away from that spot in my life, when he walked up that final fairway to his greatest victory. I vividly re-membered his ragged smile and his enthusiastic wave to the gallery surrounding the 18th green, as he made that stroll onto the front of green and into the pages of the golf history books. I was thrilled then and as I watched him, all those years removed from Augusta, I still felt that special sensation as my mind surfed back to all of those years before. I thought briefly about going over and speaking to him, but I thought better of it. Some of the great and not-so-great players do not like to be disturbed when they are at work. I let the idea go unfulfilled and continued hitting my own practice shots.

Several minutes passed and I, myself, was interrupted in my practicing by a voice, "Excuse me, but don't I know you from somewhere?" I looked up and nodded, "Yes sir, many years ago, a great many years ago actually," I replied. "It was at Augusta, wasn't it?" I replied that it was and a smile lit up his rather rugged face, tanned by many years of doing just what we were doing then, standing out in the hot sun. "I often think about that shot out of the stream." As he began to reminisce I interrupted him, "I think about it a lot too, because it was probably one of the best golf shots I have ever seen in my whole life, if not the best." As he shrugged his shoulders in a kind of humble but pleased manner, he reached out to shake my hand. "By the way," he said, "I do not owe you any money."

I felt just a bit choked-up when I heard those words and even now I am experiencing that emotion as I mentally relive that story. I found a brief moment in that time of sentiment to smile, realizing that indeed I was happy that he did not owe me any money. I was glad he had kept his promise, literally to God. We hugged each other in a moment of quietness and memory, shook hands once again, and away we both went to pursue our passion. How could I have gained a greater gift than the essence of that parable? It makes me aware every time I think about it of how grateful I am to have God and golf, both in my life.

There are times in most everyone's life when special things happen and the same can be true in one's life as it relates to golf. There are no real reasons for these events to occur, except that they are supposed to happen to us and they do. That was a special event in my golf life and in my life in general, because the two great loves in my life found a common ground on which to exist. That is power above and beyond the average day and the average course of events in anyone's life. There is, in this case, a definite and obvious tie between golf and spirituality. I was to find out more and more about that relationship as the years and rounds rolled by.

Some would have you believe that golf and the history of golf may have their conception and/or relevance, at some point, in the occult. There is nothing further from the truth, at least in my mind and heart. (We will be dealing with the subject of golf and the occult in Chapter Seventeen, as we discuss the metaphysical aspects of the game of golf.)

Yet to further make my point here, golf is not a product of the occult. Golf is a product of the light and not the darkness. If it sometimes or often seems otherwise to anyone, they should play another game. I do strongly feel that things happen, not always out of coincidence, but they happen for a reason. More later.

We have golf in our lives because it can and will create joy in our hearts and souls if we want that and allow that to happen. We search for that feeling because we need that feeling to make us feel whole. We do need to feel and have something special in our lives because those special things allow us balance against whatever negatives might come into our lives. Golf, for many people, allows that to happen. Someone who knows how to extrapolate good things from anything, is a fortunate person indeed. The same is true for someone who can receive a certain amount of goodness in their lives from golf. I do wish that for everyone who picks up a golf club—ah, but alas other things sadly appear and take center stage. Those things of a negative nature that often arise can only be attributed to ourselves and they are not the fault of God. Life is such that everything in which we are involved will not be perfect and always just as we want it to be. If it is wrong, don't blame God, fix it or get some help to fix it. If it goes in the woods and rolls into a stream, put on your rain pants and hit it out of the water, for there is victory waiting just around the dogleg.

> *There is a valley deep and green, filled with*
> *wonderful shades of the Spring.*
> *If you go into that valley you must arm yourself*
> *with courage and honor,*
> *For in that valley are all of the shadows and*
> *memories*
> *Of all of the soldiers who make the memories of*
> *that place forever great.*

CHAPTER FOUR

My Trip to Vietnam

In 1966 I joined the military and became an army chaplain. Two years later, like thousands of men and women, most of them younger than I was by at least a decade, I was sent to the war raging in Southeast Asia. I knew I would be away from my family, my friends, and of course, I would be away from golf, for at least a year, because of that little trip to Vietnam. In those years I really did love golf, as I have previously mentioned but because I did not truly understand the reality of the game, I was not in love with the pure aspects of the game of golf. In those days there were no levels of golf for me other than just the rabid desire to play the game and probably needing to play every chance I had to do so.

I looked forward to working in Vietnam because the war had created an immense need for my ministry there. I knew I would miss my family and my friends—and of course, my golf.

As one might expect I found a totally different world over there than I had ever seen, dreamed of, or known before. I spent every night but five in the jungle during my tour there, but I maintained the same ritual of exercise for golf, as I had done for many years before, back in the world. (For those military personnel who were sent to Vietnam, back in the world of course meant back in the good old U.S. of A.) I am sure that many of the troops must have thought that the chaplain was a bit crazy when they witnessed me in the evening before bedding down and in the morning, at first light, doing those weird stretching exercises. Yet when I was in the midst of doing them, they somehow kept me mentally connected to golf, when physically I was so far away from it. The truth of the matter was that I was closer than I knew, for when I checked in at my duty station on my arrival there in South Vietnam, I was introduced to my chaplain's assistant. I would have never been able to guess what I was to find out about this young man. No, he was not a golfer, probably the furthest thing from it. As a matter of fact he was not even interested in sports at all. His name was Gary Palmer. In that day and until this day the names of Gary Player and Arnold Palmer are held in the highest esteem, as they relate to professional golf. I knew that this was going to be a special time and place for me to be, even though I was so far away from the world of golf. Still I guess I was pretty close, at least to Gary and Palmer. Some would say that this was a coincidence, but I thought differently. The magic continues.

I was aboard the hospital ship SS *Hope* on one occasion, several months after my arrival in Vietnam. I was there to visit some of the wounded men from one of my units, who were being medically treated on the ship. When I finished my visiting I was standing on the helipad awaiting my ride back to the jungle and the 101st. It was then that I spotted, of all things, a golf practice net where one could hit real golf balls. It was on the rear deck of the ship and of course it peaked my interest, which is probably of no surprise to any who might have read this far or who know me. I felt like a child saying, "Can I play, please, can I play?" Strangely enough there was no one else using the practice net, so I figured, "Why not?" So I did and it felt really good, in a special kind of way that only hitting a golf ball can make one feel. I must have hit a ball or two hundred or maybe more. Several helicopters came and went and it seemed as if I had to stay for at least a few more balls.

On that beautiful afternoon, somewhere on the open sea, off the coast of Vietnam, at least for a short time, my year of golf celibacy was broken. I guess I fell off of the wagon, at least for that brief time. "It had been too long," I thought as I watched from the helicopter as the hospital ship faded into the late afternoon light. I felt a bit of a smile cross my lips and slide through my heart, when I remembered some of the old movies I had seen through the years. I recalled two people who had just finished a scene of lovemaking, of course leaving much more to the imagination than is left today, lying there together with those satisfied looks on their faces and having a smoke. I guess, had I been a smoker, I would probably have had to light up at that moment. The hospital ship SS *Hope* gave many soldiers wonderful care in those days and a gracious amount of hope. I know that on that warm afternoon it gave this chaplain hope and joy and that is for sure.

Then came that fateful day in 1969, while on an operation in the Ashau Valley, I fell victim to a land mine. As I was running down a small saddle or path on the edge of a cliff I stepped on an anti-personnel mine. The explosion hurled me down a small valley and as it did I knew just what had happened to me because I had seen it too many times before. Actually once is too many times. As I write these words, to this day, I can still remember the smell of the gunpowder from the explosion, filling my nostrils. When I finally stopped rolling and falling I looked down and the lower part of my left leg was gone. Strangely enough I had very little pain. I tried to stop the bleeding from the wound to my leg by using the boot string from my right jungle boot. How this all happened is not important, but the fact that it happened is very important to the rest of my life to this point and especially to my golf life. Soon there were other soldiers there to help me, one was a sergeant I had known for several of my months in Vietnam. "Chap, are you all right?" he asked. I guess my response to him took him by surprise. I asked him a question that will forever be burned in my memory and I would find out, many, many years later, that it was forever burned into his memory also.

I looked up at him and he looked as if he was going to cry. I grabbed his hand, squeezing it tightly and I asked, him "Sarge, how am I going to be able to play golf on one leg?"

He looked down at me and asked, "What?" I repeated the question and a slight smile crossed his parched, dirty lips and he made the statement of the hour. "Chaplain, please excuse me for saying so, but you are one crazy son of a bitch." Maybe I was, because I was not concerned about living or dying. I was not concerned about my family. I was not concerned about my profession. I guess in the back of my mind I knew all of those things would somehow be all right. As the medics were placing me on the jungle penetrater so I might be lifted up to the Medivac chopper that was noisily hovering overhead, the sergeant grabbed my hand one more time and this time with real tears rolling down his dirty cheeks, he said," Chaplain, I do not know how you will play golf on one leg, but if there is a way you will find it."

It was in those months that lay ahead when my body was trying to get its strength back that I was just screaming inside to play golf once again. I did not talk about golf to anyone because I wanted to wait and see if I was really going to be able to play again. I wanted to hold a club in my hand and feel my hand melt softly into the grip of that club. I remembered the sergeant's words as they echoed over and over in my head and, like him, I also felt way down deep inside of myself that I would find a way to play golf again, somewhere and somehow out there in those months ahead.

Then after two months of being a patient in the hospital I was granted leave from Walter Reed Army Medical Center, for the first time since my injury. I had been sent to that hospital in the first place because it was close to my home and the rehabilitation program there was supposedly good. I traveled to visit my family, my wife, my daughter, and my mother. It was good to be home and in the house where I had spent so many years as a young boy. It had been a happy home, for the most part, for my family and me.

No matter how much I thought about those boyhood yesterdays my mind just kept wandering back to golf. I would often get up and walk, with the help of my new crutches, into my old bedroom. I would take one of my clubs out of the golf bag, which now stood there in the corner of the room, just waiting to be used. I would stand on my one good leg and take a practice swing or two and then go back into the other room and think about how it was going to happen for me, one day, out there in the future—golf I mean.

I realized from the beginning that my leg was gone, I was not denying that fact. Yet my mind was busy thinking about how I was going to lick this thing. Before my injury I had never even seen an artificial limb in my whole life, so I had no way of knowing just how this new leg was going to work and how it would be for me. I was constantly trying to devise a device of my own, in my mind of course, which would rotate and allow me to swing at a golf ball properly. I even drew pictures of what I thought might be needed to get me ready to walk and play golf once again. I wanted so much to just hit the golf ball again and again.

Then on the second visit to my old home place I decided that I just had to hit a ball or fifty, so I asked my brother to put my golf clubs in the trunk of my car. "Are you going to be all right?" he asked with some concern and I told him I was going to be just fine. I drove to the local high school and walked out onto the football field with a bag full of golf balls and a pitching wedge. I stood there for a few minutes and a thousand memories came rushing back to me from many years before, when I had played football there on that same field on so many wonderful Friday nights.

"The memories are nice," I thought to myself, "but I came here to hit golf balls." I started slowly swinging the pitching wedge and standing on one foot in that late June afternoon sunshine and finally I hit my first golf shot, since the hospital ship SS *Hope* had given me hope. Standing on one leg and hitting golf balls I found out was not so great; it was tiring, but I was finally hitting golf balls once again. Yes! (That was a great day for me.)

Right there on that afternoon I was transported mentally from a place of doubt to a place where action and desire come together and form a union of joy and reality. This happened for me when the club head finally met the golf ball. After quite a while and many rest periods later my good leg was getting tired, but my spirit, I believe, was still strong and it was on fire and soaring higher than I had ever known it to soar before. I was somewhat in control of my physical nature and body once again. I was going to play golf again. "This was truly a day of resurrection for me," I thought to myself. That might sound a bit sacrilegious, but the truth of the matter is that God has never taken a backseat to golf in my life. He does not need to, for they coexist in a place that brings me joy and peace. That is why they both mean so much to me, and have for such a long time.

In the months that followed that second visit to my family home, I realized once and for all that I was indeed going to play golf again. I still had no way of knowing just what was out there ahead for me. Some nights I would lay there in my bed in the medical center and look at the strange wire contraption that was attached to my injured leg. In my wildest dreams I could not have imagined what was out there waiting for me. Along with the desire to play golf again came the new desire to understand more about this special game. That drove me to try and learn as much as I could about this attractive sport and why so many people seem to be so hooked on it. (I guess I was and am one of those people.) I was to find out that this game can take us, if we let it, to some of the most wonderful places, physically, mentally, and spiritually imaginable. I realized, at some point, in those months, that I was searching for more than a way to play again. I was also searching for the real reason that was driving me to want to play golf, period. In my searching, I was to find out many things about myself and about golf in the years that were ahead. It sounds as if I was obsessed, but the truth of the matter is I was on a mission and in the early stages of an odyssey—and I was obsessed.

What follows is one man's trek through many years of enjoying friends, places, times, and stages of emotion that I could never have imagined being possible, in all my hours of daydreaming. All of this I owe to a higher state than this great sport. Because of being in Vietnam as a chaplain and stepping on that landmine, I have truly come to better understand my passion. That time, during the war and after, set me on a course to have all of the joy, inspiration (given and received), travel, and wholesome experiences that could be the possessions of many people, let alone just one person. All of this happened to me. I have truly been blessed in more ways than I can count. A friend and a fellow Vietnam vet, who I met while we were both patients in the hospital in those early days, after our life-altering incidents in Vietnam, shared with me the following bit of prose. The words were written on the wall of the cell of a confederate soldier who was a P.O.W.

> *I asked God for strength, that I might achieve;*
> *I was made weak, that I might learn humbly to obey.*
> *I asked for health, that I might do greater things;*
> *I was given infirmity, that I might do better things.*
> *I asked for riches, that I might be happy;*
> *I was given poverty, that I might be wise.*
> *I asked for power, that I might have the praises*
>   *of men;*
> *I was given weakness, that I might feel the need of*
>   *God.*
> *I asked for all things, that I might enjoy life;*
> *I was given life, that I might enjoy all things.*
> *I got nothing that I asked for—but everything I*
>   *had hoped for.*
> *Almost in spite of myself, my unspoken prayers*
>   *were answered.*
> *I am among all men, most richly blessed.*

I am among all men, most richly blessed. That is all I can think of to say when I realize what has happened to me in my life, as it relates to this great game. I am truly and richly blessed because, one day, long ago and far away, I walked into a pawnshop and purchased a starter set of golf clubs and indeed the odyssey was on.

— CHAPTER FIVE —

Recuperating and Golf

Recuperating after my injuries in Vietnam was the major item on my agenda of things I knew I had to achieve. With that came more golf, which meant more practice and many more strengthening exercises. I found a number of people in the medical center who liked to play golf and I was back in the saddle again, so to speak, standing on one leg and hitting the golf ball. It did feel really good and satisfying. I reached a place physically where I felt as if I could at least participate in some golf tournaments. I found out about an organization by the name of the National Amputee Golf Association. I also found out their annual golf championship was to be held that summer in Grand Haven, Michigan.

My first tournament experience after the loss of my leg, was going to be a championship sponsored by amputees for amputees. I was qualified merely because I had lost my leg. When I got to the tournament in Grand Haven; people were there from all over the United States and with all sorts of limbs missing. That was the time I realized I was in a category of special people. I recall one man who had both arms off and he played with two artificial arms. I was amazed at his skill. The first day of the tournament I played in the foursome with him and he shot an

83. I was truly happy to see what could happen if one applies themselves appropriately. I remember that he had so much metal on his body that when he swung the golf club at the ball, he sounded like a tank rolling up a hill. Even with his arms missing he had confidence in himself and that I was to learn is so important.

I played, standing on my one leg, supporting myself with one of my crutches. I did not play well, but I played and that somehow was what mattered the most to me at that point. I know even today, all these years later, that just playing golf in some fashion is the highlight for me. Each day there in that Michigan sunshine I wanted to play better than I had the day before, but that did not happen; still I must emphasize the fact that I was at least playing golf again. I was a bit anxious, but in a way I was feeling contentment with what was happening with me and with my golf.

Each of the evenings while I was there in Michigan, I went to the same restaurant because I could sit out on the deck overlooking the lake. It was a calming time for me and a time to reflect and remember the day's play, and shots hit or not hit. For the first time in my life I realized I was reflecting on the golf I had played and not just thinking about playing golf again. I sat there also thinking about all the different people whom I had met and the new friends who had come my way because of this great sport. I had truly enjoyed all of the people and above all the feeling of competition, even though I was quite a bit away from being in the competition for a top twenty or so spot. Yet I was playing golf again and all I could say was, WOW!

It was at that point that I could not wait to play golf again, the next day. I felt truly blessed to be able to play golf again period, but also to find a new relationship beginning with the game, something I had not worked for or understood in those early years of playing golf. This was a far better place for me mentally, relative to golf, than I had ever known in the past. There seemed to be new and different meanings in the game for me. That was my single accomplishment in those days in western Michigan and it felt good.

I met many people during that week and as I said just a bit earlier; they had an amazing number of limbs missing, but they were doing just what they wanted to do. They were all playing golf and it seemed to me that they were truly loving the game and having fun. Everyone did not play well, but they played. I realized we were all drawn to the game of golf for different reasons. For many of those (us) gathered together there, I am sure, that at some point in their lives they must have thought that playing golf again or ever might not be possible, but not the Sarge or me. Maybe me a little bit in the beginning. "Still that was then and this is now," I thought to myself, smugly. I was blessed to be able to play golf again and to have met all of those wonderful people who were fantastic examples of courage and dedication, not only for me, but I truly believed for so many others with whom they came into contact in their everyday lives.

Some months later and with many practice shots under my belt, I was invited to play in a Pro-Am golf tournament in the Philadelphia area of Pennsylvania, at the Whitemarsh Golf Club. I was extremely excited to just be able to play on the same golf course with those great tour players, most of whom were well-known because of their great successes in the game of golf. The word had gotten around that a Vietnam veteran who had lost his leg in the war was going to be playing in that day's event. After a few warm-up shots I walked past the 18th green on my crutches, heading toward the 10th teebox, which was going to be our 1st hole of play that day and I realized that there were a number of wheelchairs situated around the back of the 18 green. I was informed that these men were also Vietnam vets, and they were all patients from the Valley Forge Army Hospital near Philadelphia. Indeed they had been told that there was a Vietnam vet and amputee playing in the day's activities, and they all wanted to come to the golf course on that day to see him play. I guess I realized they were also there to get away from the hospital and maybe to drink some beer.

When I saw them all gathered there in their wheelchairs my heart was full, nearly to the point of tears. As I passed the green I just had to stop and shake their hands. As I walked away from the greenside where they sat, toward our 1st tee, I remembered when my father had once talked to me about sentimentality.

He had said on one occasion, "Crying is not something to be ashamed of because it can be a sign of manhood." "Boy, I must really be a man," I thought to myself as I approached the 10th tee and my jump into a new way of thinking about this game of life and this game of golf. (I would remember his words many times down the road.)

Again I did not play extremely well through the first 8 holes. I did hit a few good shots here and there, but as we approached the 18th hole, I just knew that those vets in their wheelchairs would be there waiting for me. As I stood over the tee shot and then took a swing at the ball it traveled straight and true into the middle of the fairway.

As we approached the end results of our tee shots, Steve, the professional who had been stuck with our group, said to me, "I do not want to put any undue pressure on you, but you know that they are up there and they have come to see you. Give it your best shot." "Wow," I thought to myself, "what an honor this is for me." The green was an elevated one and I could not see the back of it from the fairway, but I knew that they knew I was coming up the fairway. I also knew they were up there waiting to see a shot of distinction.

What I did not realize, until much later in my life, was that they were really there to get hope and not to just see a great golf shot from me. If that sounds a bit corny, then so be it, but that was the case as I see it now, all these years later. I asked my caddie, after he finished walking off the distance from the closest yardage marker to my ball, how far it was to the middle of the green. Because of the aforementioned raised green we could not even see the flag, but I knew that it was on the front part of the green because we had observed it when we walked by the green earlier in the morning.

He handed me a 5 iron but I gave it back to him and I asked him for a 6 iron instead. He looked at me and he knew that I was feeling pumped up. I really wanted to hit a good shot, not just for me, but for them. Steve, still trying to be helpful, reminded me the pin was on the front of the green. It was like everyone was waiting and wanting me to hit a good shot. I also wanted so much to hit that good shot they had all come to see because I did not want to let down the guys behind the green. I hit the 6 iron and when I did the ball disappeared over the hill where the green was and I heard cheers. I knew I had hit a good shot. As I made my way up the hill on my crutches and onto the surface of the green I heard loud clapping and ungolf-like noises coming toward me from the direction of the wheelchairs. I did not care how ungolf-like they were, because they were sounds of joy and pride and that made me happy. I was probably smiling and maybe even feeling a bit of pride myself, as I stood and looked at where my ball had stopped on the green. I guess pride can be bad, but at that moment it felt good, dare I say wonderful.

My ball had come to rest at the top of the green, 40 to 45 feet above where the flagstick was located. When I saw where the golf ball had finally stopped I was glad I had not hit the 5 iron or some of the wheelchairs might have come into play. I had hit a good shot because the mark left by the golf ball on the green was only about 7 or 8 inches from the cup. I repaired the ball mark near the pin and walked up the undulation to where my ball had finally stopped. As I looked at the putt I was facing, I realized it was downhill on a slick green.

My first thought was that I did not want to hit the ball so hard when I putted it that it would go past the hole and off of the green and then down the steep hill again. After getting some help from my caddie, who told me not to hit the ball so hard it would roll off the green, I smiled and told him I had already thought about that. I approached the putt and took one more short glimpse at the line of the putt and then I addressed the ball. I placed the stump of my left leg over the handle of my metal crutch for balance and looked down at the PING putter face. I could hear faint voices from the direction of the wheelchairs talking to me, urging me on.

Normally that would be distracting to a golfer, but somehow those voices were just about what I needed at that time. They gave me comfort, confidence, and a definite sense of mission. I just did not want the ball to roll completely off of the green. As the putter face struck the ball I heard those voices from behind me encouraging me, "Come on, Chap. Come on, Chap." From the moment the ball came off of the putter face, I had a feeling that it was going to softly roll right down that slippery slope and fall into the hole. It seemed as if that would be the only thing that would have made that time any more perfect. As the ball started its long trek, the voices from the perimeter of the green grew louder and louder. The ball never wavered and when it reached the hole it dove right into the center of the cup. I remember what my thoughts had been prior to that putt, "Please make me an example."

As I said before I have never invoked God's help in my golf game, but I have received it more times than I will even know, even without asking. I have asked for companionship and like that day at Whitemarsh, I have received it and have had those prayers answered. He has granted me that and much, much more. I wanted to make that putt so badly, not just because we all want to make our putts, but I wanted to make it for those guys who were there rooting for me, for their pride and their spirit. All of that might sound flowery, but I do not care. That is what I wanted and why I wanted it and I would feel that way over and over again in my life.

I recall to this day the cold arms of those wheelchairs, but the oh so warm handshakes and embraces that greeted me as I approached the veterans, behind the green, after everyone else had finished putting out. It seemed that the script had been written and the story was told just the way that it should have been told, for everyone involved. Steve, our professional, said as we finally walked away from the green toward the 1st hole—to continue what could only be a boring finishing 9, after the past ten minutes or so, "That was great timing and above all a memory that will last me my entire lifetime. I think you had a little help from behind the green and above the green. What do you think, Chap?" I was rather full of emotion so I shook my head in agreement, because he was correct on both counts.

As I recalled that putt over and over again in the days that followed, I knew it would be almost impossible to sink that putt again, but I also knew that wonderful things can and will happen to us in this wonderful game of life and the game of golf. I also realized that I did not have to ever make that particular putt again because I made it at the appropriate time, for all concerned. I knew that it would be hard to go through a feeling sequence such as the one I have just described, but I was to find out in the years ahead that those feeling levels are not impossible to attain. They just keep on coming.

I know without a doubt, good things happen to us. I also know that sometimes they are outside of our control. I am glad of that because they can happen to any of us, who are able to open ourselves up for these events to become part of our lives.

There are days when all we have to do is get up
And wonderful gifts are given to us.
A walk in the warmth of the sunshine
With a good friend or two
A chance to test our metal against nature
And a chance to be, as we should, to those about us.
The sad part would be to miss all of that.

— CHAPTER SIX —

Letterman Army Hospital (Golf Clinics)

Through the years of playing golf I have often thought about the wonderful sense of sharing that golf has created in my life with so many different kinds of people. My first duty station, after my rehabilitation at Walter Reed Army Hospital in Washington, D.C., was in San Francisco at the Letterman Army Medical Center, inside the gates of the famous and now former Presidio Army Base. What a beautiful spot it was and still is! It sits right on shore of the San Francisco Bay with a wonderful view of the city on one side and a fabulous view of the bay on the other. From nearly everywhere on these historic grounds one can sit and watch as the fog rolls in over the Golden Gate Bridge and fills the bay with its own special brand of feelings. The hospital building was a brand-new structure when I arrived there. There were some disturbing items of similarity between that hospital and the one I had just come from. There were too many wounded soldiers. Of course, one was too many, but the war was still raging in Southeast Asia and the wounded were coming to us daily.

Late one night, as I was driving home from work over the Golden Gate Bridge and thinking just how good golf had been to me and how much it had helped me when I was wounded, I came up with an idea. I would endeavor to see if it might be feasible to start a golf program for the amputees who were patients there in the hospital. There was a perfect space to teach golf out behind the hospital where I myself had hit many a practice shot, instead of going to lunch or doing other things. Does that sound familiar? The following day I approached a couple of the orthopedic doctors with this idea and they were enthused about the possibilities of such a project. They felt that anything that would make the guys get out of their beds and into their wheelchairs and moving around was a good idea indeed.

After about a month or so of inviting the amputees to come and participate in this idea of mine, one or two of them finally did come to investigate just what was going on out there behind the hospital. The reality is they probably came to get me off of their backs. No matter, they came and after the word got around that we were not having church services on the back lawn of the medical center, then even more of the young amputees began to come out and participate. It was fun for them, but it was truly thrilling for me. I loved watching their faces almost glow as they would stand on one foot and swing at the golf ball, sometimes hitting the ball and sometimes missing it completely. Some of them even fell down, while the others enjoyed a laugh at their expense. Still it seemed that the fallen always got up to try again to hit still another shot that would more often than not make them happy. They even started competing against each other to see who could hit the golf ball better, straighter, and farther. It was good to see the male ego being aroused again. The testosterone was flowing.

With the program growing, and the need for equipment growing also, there was a need for some space to store all of the equipment, much of which had been donated to the hospital by one of the local golf professionals from the Olympic Golf Club. I petitioned one of the officers in the medical center for a locker at the back entrance of the patient building to store the equipment near where we were using it. He refused to sign off on the authorization for the use of an otherwise empty locker. Instead of acting like I wanted to, I invited him to come out to one of the teaching sessions. He himself was a golfer of sorts. On the day he decided to come and see just what was really going on, the weather was beautiful and there were about six young guys out there, including a young man named Jim, who had lost both of his legs and an arm.

As I watched this young man make his way toward the group, I recalled the first time that I had ever seen him. He, of course, was lying there in his bed on the fourth floor of the hospital. He looked as if he was about to die. He had been losing weight since his injuries and of course his wounds were severe and evident. As I got to know him better and better, I did invite him out on several occasions to watch the guys hit some golf shots. I was sincerely hoping that as he gathered more and more strength he would be ready to try some golf shots himself. I remembered how bitter and depressed he was and how I thought that his emotions were indeed adequate for the circumstances surrounding him. He got angry with me in the beginning because I would try to encourage him to come out and join in with the others. A number of times when I went into see him he would intentionally roll away from me to face the wall or the door, depending on which side of the bed I was standing.

As the months rolled by Jim began to regain some of his strength and he was able get around a little better in his wheelchair. I often glanced from the practice area up toward the glassed-in solarium on the fourth floor and he would be sitting there in his wheelchair and peering down at the other amputees hitting golf balls and having fun. I knew in my heart that one day he would be down there with the other patients. That day occurred when the colonel had come by to see just what was going on out on the back lawn of the medical center. My little friend from Idaho, one arm and all, was there in attendance.

I had always been so moved by the sheer delight that the amputees got from just hitting a golf ball. I realized early on that what might seem to be little to those of us who are relatively healthy, could actually mean a great deal to someone who thought that sports might have been out of the question for them, taking into account their physical situation and condition. Twenty yards might be trite and even trivial to you and me, but to someone else that short distance and just the swinging of the golf club could bring a smile to their sometimes smileless faces and a large lump in the throats of those of us who might be watching their joy and unbridled enthusiasm. But that is what this game can do for anyone...

Jim was there for his first day with the group. I realized, as I watched him, that he had changed a great deal in the months since I first met him. He was still thin, but he was gaining weight instead of losing it. At first when I asked him to try a swing at the golf ball he did not want any part of that. Still I knew, just as I had known when I watched him looking down from the fourth floor, that sooner or later he would be a part of this golf clinic and he and I would both be glad that he was. After much encouraging from most of the other amputees gathered there and of course from me, he decided that he would give a swing a try. I watched him, with a little help from two of the other patients, roll his wheelchair over the short distance to the grassy area that was used for those lessons. I thought how pale and undernourished he still looked. The colonel was standing behind everyone just watching what was going on. He was in his full uniform and the sun was making him warm; of that, I was sure. I was also sure that what he was seeing was also making him more than just a bit uncomfortable.

We removed the side handles of the wheelchair and Jim took the 9 iron in his hand with a certain amount of trepidation. I was aware of that. He locked the brakes on the wheelchair and then he slid up to the front of the chair, preparing for his maiden voyage. I showed him the almost proper way to hold the club. He took a few small swings in my direction and then he tried to hit the little white ball, which I had placed on a tee for him. He missed the ball completely and then he missed it again and then on his third try he dribbled one off of the tee. That brought a slight smile to his slender face, which seemed to be more about embarrassment than joy. What happened next changed the lives of most everyone gathered there.

He took another swing at the teed-up ball and with his one good hand he actually hit the ball and it flew about 15 yards and the expression on his face changed from uncertainty to joy and it was worth a million dollars to me. No, as the MasterCard commercial says, it was indeed priceless for us all. He smiled as he watched the ball fly and then he broke out into a big laugh. His face no longer looked tired. It was the first time I had seen him really smile or laugh since he had arrived at Letterman Hospital. His blue eyes, though still recessed back in his head, seemed to just sparkle and shine. I witnessed a great metamorphosis take place right there before my eyes. All I could say was, "Thank you, God, and thank you, golf, for this special day." There is a close relationship in the peace they both can and will provide, if we are willing to allow that to happen.

In the middle of this true time of pure joy, I glanced back over my shoulder at the colonel and there he stood, in the hot afternoon sun, with tears streaming down his face, as he watched the young man smile and then laugh. The young man's chest even seemed to swell with a bit of true and good pride as the others there gathered around him and offered their approval with a long and loud round of applause. I remember hearing the young man say as the applause ended, "I would get up and take a bow, but you know."

Everyone laughed because they all knew that he could not stand up and because he was feeling better about himself and his situation, good enough even to make a rather light comment about his own physical condition and situation. The colonel left without any comment of his own to anyone gathered there and yet the tears said it all, as did his red face and that white tear-stained handkerchief, which he stuck in his pants pocket as he walked briskly away. The golf program got a large locker the following day and life went on, in a good way, for all of us gathered there on that beautiful day, and Jim hit more and more good golf shots.

I thought that day, as I was driving home and I am still thinking now, as I write these words, "It is not a coincidence that my work and my play go hand and heart together." The young man is still in my memory, as I recall the times that he and the others truly enjoyed themselves out there behind the hospital hitting a little white golf ball. I can still see Jim's wonderful wide smile and his glowing blue eyes as he watched the golf ball take flight. It is amazing how many people from all walks of life, of all stations in life, and in many parts of this world can and have found not only joy in this great game, but also peace. I have, through the years, received letters from a number of those amputees who learned their early rudimentary golf skills right there behind the hospital. I have played golf with many of them through the years and I have to smile with some secret pride whenever that happens. One of them even went on to find himself a job in the golf business. Yet my favorite letter came from my little timid friend from Idaho. He explained in his letter that he had not yet completely mastered the game of golf, but he was still trying. He informed me that the greatest thrills he had felt since his return from the war was the feeling of being able to finally sit in his wheelchair and hit a golf ball. His final statement on the subject was, "Down in my stomach I just love to hit that little white ball, when I do." I understand that....Many others do also.

On occasions I proudly look at quite a number of photos that were taken out behind the hospital—of the guys hitting golf balls on one leg, no legs, with one arm—and they all have one thing in common, they are all smiling. They were all having fun in the midst of a great deal of crap that was coming down on them and in their lives because of what had happened to them in the war. They started golf for all of the right reasons. It allowed them to be free in a way that they had not experienced before. *They were having fun.*

I have a photo taken at an amputee tournament in 1978. Five out of the six division winners in that competition were amputees from Letterman Army Hospital and that grassy knoll overlooking the San Francisco Bay. I remember how proud of them I was as the photo was snapped and they (we) were all smiling and happy.

As I said before, one of those then young men, who by now like us all has found a way to get a bit older, decided to seek a career in the golf industry. I must say that makes me feel that those sessions out behind the hospital truly had long-lasting effects, at least for him. Many young men came back from that war and they got displaced, but Mark, he got placed. That place is great. The joy that is mine today, relative to the joy those physically challenged young men felt because of golf, will forever be a gift that I will cherish the rest of my life.

> *Climb that mountain if you must*
> *And gather strength as up you go,*
> *For once the journey begins,*
> *Pain will cease and joy will not fail to find you.*

CHAPTER SEVEN

Attitudes

Proper attitudes are not only important in everything we do, but they are also necessary for us to have in order to make it through every day of our lives in a positive fashion. Like with most things there are good attitudes and of course there are bad attitudes. It is sometimes easy for us as human beings to forget good attitudes people exhibit and it's hard to forget a declaration or an exhibiting of a bad attitude. If our own outlooks and attitudes are good ones, we can more easily remember other people's good attitudes. Conversely bad attitudes are usually remembered no matter what our own personal attitude might be. Attitudes are just an example, a mirrored image, of who we are inside. In other words they reflect just who we really are way down deep.

Often the way we approach the game of golf is the same way we approach our everyday lives. Quite often we exhibit the same attitude in all of the aspects of our lives that we take to our daily golf outings. There can be exceptions to that rule, of course, with the person, who for whatever reason, finds the rest of his or her life quite different from the viewpoint of caring and satisfaction than they do their golf game or whatever that artery of release might be. These people can be one way emotionally at home and emotionally another way at work or at play. They do present a definite attitude to their family, friends, and fellow workers, be it good or bad. Each of those attitudes could well be different for some people, although more times than not our attitudes do carry over into everything we are involved in.

Let's dwell for just a bit on this game of golf and the attitudes that might be prominent in the lives of some golfers. Every person, who has played this great game, can remember a time or two or maybe more when he or she felt so angry, so frustrated, and so completely lost that there were feelings and emotions of hatred floating around in their head and heart, as those feelings related to the game of golf. How many people say or have said about golf, in their lives, "I hate this game." If that has not happened to you, then two things come immediately to my mind. The first is *we* are in the minority. The second is we have seen this kind of behavior from someone with whom we have played golf at sometime and place in our recent golf past.

It is obvious that one person's attitude quite often differs from some other people's attitude, with whom they might be associated, merely because people differ in their approach to life, family and everything else. That of course includes golf. Does that theory ring a bell? If you cannot remember a day in your golf life when you felt as if you got absolutely no good breaks whatsoever, then once again you must understand that you are in a small and unique minority. It is a part of human nature that allows people to be consumed by anger and frustration. When this happens tempers rise to a point of throwing clubs, and any other objects that are within reach and movable. Bad shots and bad breaks will continue to occur, as do good breaks and good shots. Still for some people golf has never been something to seethe over or something to be angry about.

For these people there are too many points of joy and happiness in golf to waste time being angry about the few bad parts of their trek through life with golf. There is truly too much in and about this great sport to make us happy for us to waste time being unhappy about some passing moment of emotional pain. Please understand also that we all do have our moments, but they can pass as quickly as they came on. They can change with just the next swing of the golf club. So it is with many people who play this game. A good shot or a good break or bounce can change us from whiners to pleasant people—and maybe even winners.

A few years back, I was nearly hit by a flying golf club that had been thrown by a fellow competitor in a prominent golf tournament. He got so angry at the turn of events in his day and in his round of golf that he threw one of his golf clubs, and in my direction. I came as close that day, as any other time in my entire life, to striking someone. I thought his actions were not only dangerous, but they were childish, and his behavior was unbecoming of anyone who plays this wonderful game.

I walked over to where he was standing and grabbed him by the collar of his yellow golf shirt and explained to him just what I was thinking. I also told him I was going to report his actions to the tournament committee and to the sponsorship of the event in which we were playing. I further explained that if he needed to act out in that particular fashion in the future maybe he should consider being involved in some other sport such as the WWF. If this grand game debilitates us to a point of anger at this level then we should never play it again.

There have been times in my golf life when I have refused to play with people who lose their tempers and act like some spoiled child, moaning and groaning about how much they dislike or even hate this game of golf. I do not want to hear this nonsense about something I love, nor do I need this in the serenity of my golf time. There have also been times in the past when playing golf with friends, that I have seen some of them slam their clubs into the ground in frustration and speak a few harsh words or maybe more than a few, which by the way are not worthy of repeating in these lines. All I can do is laugh when this happens because I know that they love this game and like everyone else, it gets the best of most of them sometimes.

I hope for more of those days in the future, not because of the anger, but because that means my friends and I will be together again, which I might add, is a major fun part of the whole process of this game. You see I know these people and I like these people. Many of us are young in our minds and childish in our quest for perfection even though our bodies have reached maturity, as has for many of us our level of achievement in the game of golf. I am sure the man I mentioned earlier, in the yellow shirt, also has friends who care for him and are able to overlook his temper flare-ups. I have been told, "to err is human, to forgive divine." I forgave him, but I did not want to play golf with him, ever again, nor have I.

The truth of the matter is that attitudes are what separate golfers of distinction from the regular golfers of the masses. This, by no means, is meant to imply that great golfers, those we see on television each week, never lose their tempers or find themselves out of control. The opposite is usually the case and I know that for a fact. Some of them get so mad that they wish hexes on themselves, their golf clubs, and their caddies. They probably have said more times than they can remember, "I hate this game," but we all know that they in fact do not hate the game of golf, instead they really love it. All of this most probably goes along with the fire they have in their bellies for this game and the competitive juices they feel flowing inside of themselves when they play it.

The difference between the truly great player and the player who cannot control his emotions beyond the moment is quite simple. The truly great player is able to let the bad break, the bad decision, the distraction that brought about the anger in the first place, go. He knows that it will only get worse if he hangs on to it. Those who learn to let the negatives go survive and those who do not are "also rans." For them all of their seething can only push them and their scores further down the leader board. The same is true in life. If we hang on to those things that upset us they will only fester and send us further down the leader board of life.

When I was in the military, as I eluded to earlier, one of my commanding officers was a colonel, a man with a bad disposition as far as his attitude was concerned. Most likely by this time you will probably think that all of the colonels I encountered in the army were not the nicest people on the planet, but the opposite is actually true. Like I mentioned earlier sometimes it is only human to remember the bad items in life and forget about the good things.

We have already discussed this, but it is never harmful to have little reminders of the obvious things in our lives. This particular officer found out that I liked golf and he, shortly after I was assigned to Letterman Hospital, invited me to play golf each Wednesday with two other colonels and himself. The idea of getting away every Wednesday afternoon to play golf with these men was filled with a number of good possibilities, but it turned out that the drama was not. It seemed that every week it was the same old story. He, the colonel, would arrive at the 1st tee and we would go through the same dialogue we had done the week before. It finally became a joke to me, but it was always the same question, "How many shots do I get?" Every person who reads this will remember either asking that same question of someone or being ask that question time and time again by one of their playing partners or friends. The answer I gave to him is the same one I have used for the past thirty years. "What is your handicap?" For me that has always simplified the situation and the process.

Indeed on each of those Wednesdays the lyrics and dialogue were always the same, as was the plot and the result of every outing. I gave him the shots he deserved, according to his handicap and mine and I beat him. He would then openly complain to everyone in the surrounding area about having lost four dollars to me. Then the next week, like clockwork, he would call again and the scenario would repeat itself.

On one occasion I met him on the 1st tee as usual and the same diatribe started. This time he informed me that he needed more strokes because he did not think I was a 6 handicapper. He was implying that my handicap was wrong. I informed him that the problem was not that I was not a 6 handicapper, but the problem was rather that he was not a 12 handicapper. I told him that he was really a higher handicapper than what he always said he was. I also told him that on that day I was going to give him a stroke a hole and I was going to beat him like a drum and when the round was over I would never ever play golf with him again. I explained to him that the reason for this decision on my part was that he was not a nice person to be around and I will not allow my golf to be desecrated by anyone's bad feelings or negative attitudes.

It is difficult for me to try to explain just how mad this man got with me. His face turned red and the veins in his neck were protruding. I thought for a brief moment he was going to have a stroke. He sat in the cart beside me for the first 2 holes and never said a word to anyone. When the time came for him to hit his 1st tee shot he did so and then sat right back down in the golf cart. By the time the 2nd hole was over he was already two down. Then abruptly, as we approached the teebox of the 3rd hole, he jumped out of the golf cart and removed his golf bag from the golf cart in which we were riding and placed it on the other golf cart. From that point on I had a new riding partner in my golf cart. The rest of the day the colonel was quiet.

I really did beat him like that proverbial drum. I would not mention this, but it brought some amount of solace to me at that point. Yes, I guess you could say that I really enjoyed the feelings I was having because of that simple victory. He, as usual, griped and complained about the loss, but for me it was over and I mean truly over. One of the players in the group mentioned to me later that maybe I should have allowed him to win and I thought that was truly a sick approach to the whole situation. I guess the victory seemed kind of tainted being that the situation was what it was, although it still felt really good to put the hammer down on his bad attitude. Still I felt my day of golf was ruined to some extent by the bad feelings, and the victory would not wash those negative feelings away. Those were the thoughts that were running through my head when I drove home later that day as the sun was beginning to set into the Pacific.

On the next Tuesday the colonel had his aide telephone me and give me the tee time for our usual game the following day. I informed the major, who had called me, of what had transpired the week before. Furthermore I told him that I would not be playing any more golf with his boss. The major said to me, "but Chaplain, the colonel writes your efficiency report. This might be reflected on your military record and your future in the Army might be affected by a bad efficiency report." My reply was something that has, for many years, been a part of my thinking, "I feel more importantly that it will affect my golf game and everyone should have their priorities." The major knew that his boss was a man who had not made many friends in the hospital, because of his attitude and yet the following day he telephoned me again to see if I had, by any chance, changed my mind. Again I refused, saying to him that I would only play golf with people I like in social situations. That was that, as far as I was concerned. You might think that it was a hard line to draw, but whatever your hobbies might be, whether they are golf, fishing, reading, or hiking, you do not want the time you have set aside to follow those dreams or loves to be spoiled by some negative outside source.

The months passed and I did not play golf with the colonel, nor did I get an invite to do so again. The downside of that was, I was now working again on Wednesday afternoons. I did not even see the colonel around the hospital. During that period of time I received a telephone call from an officer in the Pentagon asking if I would be available to play a round of golf with the Undersecretary of the Army when he made an official visit to the Presidio. He informed me the foursome, which was already set up for that particular day, included the aforementioned colonel. I told the officer that I felt extremely honored by his kind invitation, but I regrettably would have to decline the invitation if the colonel was part of the foursome. I explained to him that I found his company unpleasant and not worthy of a day off to spend on the golf course. I guess I less than graciously declined.

The next day the officer called again from Washington and asked if I would play golf, with the group at the Presidio Golf Course, if the aforementioned colonel was replaced. I felt sort of bad, but I did accept the invitation under those conditions. They replaced the colonel and I readied myself for a shower of negativeness from the group on the following Monday morning.

I arrived at the golf course a bit early on the day of the golf match. It was Monday and the golf course was normally closed on Mondays, but they had opened it just for this special three-some plus me. The Undersecretary was gracious and right up front with me when I was introduced to him. When I shook his hand he asked me why I would not play golf with that particular officer and again I explained my situation to him.

I merely told him that golf, for me, was too special to have it spoiled by a situation and/or a person who was not worthy of this great sport. He explained to me that he thought I might have been a bit rigid in my approach to this particular situation. I agreed that he was probably right and his only comment to me was, "Good, and by the way you are my partner today. So play well." That was truly the end of that part of the colonel's story, yet I would be less than remiss if I left it at that.

Some months passed and my less than favorite colonel was brought into the hospital as a patient with a medical problem that was going to require some extensive surgery. To further explain what kind of attitude and personality problems this man had, the Catholic Chaplain would hesitate before going to see him. I guess he was asking for courage, even though the man was Catholic and had been his entire life, to that point. His reputation was well-known throughout the entire medical center. One day, as I was sitting in my office, I found myself thinking about him up there in that hospital room trying to keep up a brave facade. I decided I would go up to his room and visit him.

When I entered his room, he seemed a bit cold at first and I understood why. I had been hard on him, but for just reasons, at least in my biased mind.

We talked about his family and his hospitalization and of course his upcoming medical and surgical procedures. We never mentioned golf and that was probably the best thing not to talk about at that point. There were probably bad memories for both of us hiding there.

Soon after his surgery was over I went in to see him a couple of times and his attitude was somewhat better, at least it seemed so to me. He was different somehow, maybe because he seemed more mellow and even smaller lying there in the bed. I found myself laughing to myself that maybe he was still under the anesthesia they had used on him during his surgery. He was different and it was also obvious to other people.

I remember going to see him on one occasion, just before he was scheduled to go home from the hospital for a time of convalescence. He was smiling as I walked through the door of his room. I remember thinking I should check the name on the door to see if this was indeed the correct room, because I never remember him smiling too many times in my direction before that day. I guess some of that could have been my fault. After a nice, but short visit I said to him words I thought would never cross my lips, at least in his direction, "When you get up and start feeling better I think we should try to play golf together sometime." He looked surprised and I continued, "Because this is a different man than the one I knew before he had surgery. I think whatever was negative in there, they removed it in the operating room."

As much as I had thought that we never would, we did play golf again and it was fun. Above all else it was positive, as golf and all of the times we get to play this game, alone or with someone else, should be. Golf is too special to feel otherwise. There is nothing really mystical about this story, but it does hold fast to two important issues for me personally. The first is, that in golf and in life, one should be happy in doing and having both. The second is, we should always be open to change to make both of these entities better and more enjoyable. Sometimes all of us need bits of change in our lives to be better at and in what we do—work, play, or whatever.

Each of us and our attitudes are formed from objects and situations, both from our surroundings and the elements that develop deep inside ourselves from various other sources. Our attitudes, which have their genesis in our own personal history, should be explored and some sense of understanding developed about them before we make judgments about other people's attitudes. We should also examine our own attitudes even more closely than we do the attitudes of other people. That goes for the way we act in our lives and in our golf. Both of these commodities are too valuable to mess up with a negative approach to either of them.

I am sure that most people who read these words have run across some person who seemingly is always late for everything and that includes, of course, tee times. Tardiness is an attitudinal problem. Tardiness fortunately is not like cleanliness or next to godliness. The people who are constantly late for tee times do not have the same feelings for golf as those of us who burn inside to just get out there and play this great game. Some years ago I had a golf acquaintance who was late for everything—including his golf dates. On one occasion he telephoned me at my office to inquire if I was going to play golf that afternoon. When he found out that indeed my plan was to do so and I had only two other players in the group, he asked if he might join us. I invited him to do so and gave him our tee time.

We were on the teebox, getting ready to hit our drives, when he finally came hurriedly driving by the 1st tee. He yelled from his car for us to wait for him. He then had to find a parking place, go into the locker room, change his clothes and shoes, and the beat goes on and on. He caught us on the 3rd tee and he was angry, to say the least. He sulked for 15 holes but I never mentioned his tardiness to him until we had finished our round.

A short time later standing in the pro shop, I told him, "If you have to be late in the future for a tee time or anything you are doing with me, then you call me and let me know. There are other people to consider here beside yourself. You do this all of the time and it is not only frustrating for those of us left standing and waiting, but it is a controlling device. I will not put up with it any more." From that point on he was never again late when doing anything with me. Was he late in dealing with other people? Probably. This kind of behavior comes from attitude. Bad attitudes and golf are not good bedfellows.

There are also those whom we might encounter in this great and wonderful sport who are almost obsessed with the game. No, they are truly obsessed. If you are thinking about your own relationship with golf, as you read this, then read on. Obsession is an attitude all its own. Obsession is an approach to the game of golf that actually violates the peaceful reasons and strong principles for playing the game of golf. People who know me and who know of my love for this game, will laugh when they read this, because many of them think I am obsessed with the game. But the reality is I am not obsessed with it, I am in love with it. It stirs positive passion in and for me. Those who know me well will understand this. Obsession is a dark word, a dark presence, and a dark state of mind. It has a negative and dark side. Love on the other hand is a joyous sunrise kind of relationship. If that sounds poetic and/or trite then you need to reevaluate your concepts of this game and the obsessions you may or may not have with it or other things in your life, such as your family, your friends, and your profession.

Obsessions can cause marriages to collapse. They can bring businesses to ruin. They can cause deep depression and bring people to the brink and over the brink of bankruptcy, financially and emotionally. It is necessary to understand that an obsession with golf is no different from any other obsession and it can cause all of the above to happen in our lives. It can sneak up on us quietly and quickly. I know situation after situation of that being true in the lives of people whom I have known and still maintain a relationship with, relative to golf. Golf should give us good things and that is the direction it should take us. If golf, or anything else for that matter, takes or drives other good things away from us then we should examine the reasons we have to keep playing the game or being involved in whatever we are involved in. The game of golf should give to us and not take away from us. If it takes away then we have allowed it to direct our lives. We have allowed it to control our lives and that qualifies as an obsession.

Attitudes make all the difference in the world to any object of our affections. Betting on a game of golf is an attitude. Some people can take the stroll with the golf bag on their back, without a small or large wager in tow and they are as happy as they can be just being there in the outdoors and playing golf. This is true because of where they are, what they are doing, and with whom they are spending their mornings or afternoons. This not is to imply that betting is a negative thing between friends, although it can be. The bottom line is that these friends should be able to take the stroll together, without the need for the added incentive of money or drinks or whatever. There are people in my golfing life with whom the mention of a bet has never arisen or been an issue.

On the other hand there are people with whom I play, who cannot play without a wager of some sort, be it large or small. The bet should be secondary to the time spent together, doing something that is wonderful and pleasurable. The wager can and often does change one's approach to the game being played, because of the possibility of winning and/or losing. When we bet, the game plan changes because no longer is the desired end of the golf round to beat the course and par, but the game is now to beat the opponents and not lose any money or bragging rights to them, be they silent bragging rights or otherwise. Some people play much better under the pressure of a bet, while others cannot play their best for money. Some people just like or dislike the pressure that comes from the wager, large or small, and the bragging rights that do accompany victory.

The reason I believe this is an attitude situation as it relates to golf, is that I am aware of relationships that have been welded together through years of friendship and respect in golf, that have found a way to end over a lousy 5-dollar wager. I have seen relationships dissolve over a small wager, won or lost, when some torrid argument followed a round of golf. I have lost respect for some people when I have seen them get into a volatile disagreement about some trivial nonsense that has nothing to do with the real reasons we should be playing this game. The weird part in all of this is that these people cannot play together without betting on the game and the betting often causes them disharmony. This is a strange dichotomy golf alone offers us. Yet the sport here is not the villain, but rather (dare I say it?) the sportsman is the problem.

Attitudes are for many the reason these people play the game of golf and attitudes are also the reason so many people get ulcers from something that can and should bring them so much excitement and joy. That again is true in life, as well as in golf.

I do not want to imply, in any way, that in my golf life or in my life in general that my attitude has not been tested, because it has been many times. I might add though that my attitude has never broken down to the point where I have overlooked the real reason for my relationship with this game or with my work or life itself. When I drive across the Golden Gate Bridge every morning, going to work, I never fail to enjoy the magnificent beauty of that place and the serenity of that time. Nor do I fail to say thank you. So it is with golf; I may get upset at it briefly sometimes until I realize what caused the momentary lapse. Still as I said earlier, it quite often passes with the next good shot. We just need to take a look at what we have and how blessed we are to have and enjoy golf for what it is, a wonderful game.

I am not opposed to rules being interjected into this game because we have them to give the game of golf a compass and course. Still sometimes the average player can go to the extreme in interrupting them. Most of the time that comes from a need to win a match or just to win those valuable bragging rights. Someone through the years developed the rules of golf for a reason. That reason is simply to prevent chaos and maintain order in the game of golf. I am sure that through the years I have broken the rules and was not aware of those transgressions. Those faults are human and many times they come about because of a personal lack of knowledge about the rules themselves. Often these overlooking of the rules are misconstrued as cheating and that may be what it is or it just might be someone not wanting to be so strict. All of this needs to be taken into consideration when people are playing together and there may be a wager on the line.

Then the rules have to govern that day's play. I play occasionally with a professional golfer. He never plays anyone for money or even drinks. He always moves the ball around in the fairway and the rough with his clubface before he hits it, to get a better lie. I consider that his business, even though the summer rules are in effect on the golf course. He breaks the rules, but there is no one involved in that whole event and process, but himself. He is doing what he feels he wants and needs to do and he alone is affected.

I want to mention a subject that should never be mentioned when we talk about golf, and that is cheating. I will not dwell long on this subject because it can take away the beauty the game offers us. If someone intentionally cheats, he or she cheats himself or herself out of the real reasons they have to play the game of golf. Most often when a person cheats it is done to win a match or to beat the game by using shortcuts instead of practice and patience. There is no excuse for cheating.

There have been occasions when I have seen people break the rules of golf and have made a personal choice not to mention the violation until later because the game was the most important item in that particular scenario and we were not in a tournament. Most of the time I try to find a positive manner in which to bring the rule infraction to the person's attention. I have used the old, "If you are playing in a tournament and this situation occurs be careful that this particular rule is not broken." My intent is to cause no hurt feelings and this approach might allow some growth and help to occur. There have been other times when I have had to come right out and say to the person that what they were doing was not abiding by the rules and we took it from there. That is why I keep a USGA Rules book in my golf bag at all times and it is upgraded each year.

I have called rules on players in competition and on occasion I have had rules called on me. That is the reason for having rules and a governing body to develop those rules and oversee them, in the first place. One year in the British Open Hale Irwin called a rule on himself, causing a penalty of one stroke to be assessed against him. He eventually lost the British Open, yes, by one stroke. He made that call on himself because that is the way the game should be played and has to be played. He understood the rules of golf and the reasons for having them in the first place. He respected both the game and the rules. I am sure he just hated the fact that he had broken one of the rules, but he understood just what had happened and he had a true reverence for the game he loves. He did what was ethical and correct.

In this game we should never be driven by a fear of failure or a desire to win at all costs. The cost to carry that out is ultimately too high. That attitude is the same one we so often use in our marriages and with our children and in our workplace. This is play. This is recreation and not re-creation. For far better than 99% of the people who play this game it is only recreation and that is all it will ever be. That is all right too because that is why it was developed all those years ago in the rolling lands of Scotland. The quicker people with golf clubs understand the fact that this is only a game the better off they will be. For those people (most of us), recreation is all golf will ever be. Enjoy it for what it is, a game. Oh yes it is probably the best one going, but it is, in reality, only a game. If we have to be driven by something, as we participate in the game of golf, be driven by the sheer specialness of the great mental, physical, and spiritual aspects and challenges of this great and truly wonderful game.

People's attitudes are created and developed by this game as much as by life itself. Good attitudes and great expectations are where heroes in golf are born. We must always remember that good attitudes and great expectations can and do also come to the 24 handicapper, because that is the nature of this beautiful beast. In this game we have either asked it ourselves or heard it from one of our playing companions, more times than we can count, "Why me? What have I done to deserve this?" My answers to those questions are following in the next chapter. The answer is positive and easy to come by without a great amount of deep philosophical searching and thought. We are most fortunate.

The words, "The universe forces those who live in it to understand it," come to my mind at this point. We may not all understand the game of golf or even want to understand it, yet it causes most of us to try—even though few of us succeed in the total understanding of this game we call golf. Still, in a way, we succeed if we merely attempt to play the game. We are blessed to be a part of it and we should have an attitude about the game that is commensurate with the chance we have to play it, and the stature of the game itself. This can and should happen no matter what one's level of skill might be.

We need to understand only a few of the possibilities of what this game can do for us and where it can take us, mentally and physically, as well as spiritually, to truly accomplish and hold on to a great attitude, as it relates to golf and to life. Remember that few things in our lives can make our attitudes better than golf can and will, if we can approach it as we should.

> *To understand oneself is rare gift.*
> *To understand others is quite often easier,*
> *For their faults are magnified*
> *While ours are diminished, at least in our own eyes.*
> *The secret is to love both*
> *And work from wherever we are*
> *And with whatever we have*
> *To make both of them more perfect.*

— CHAPTER EIGHT —

Why Me?

I will ask the question yet again, How many times have we asked or have we heard someone else loudly ask "Why me?" when a golf ball we hit or they hit lands in the water? How many times have we asked the same question when a golf ball we hit bounces out of bounds or plugs in the face of a greenside bunker? It is not unusual for golfers to reach a point where they feel as if they never seem to get a good hop or bounce—or a break, other than one of a negative nature. I have heard words yelled from playing partners that would paint the air blue, if indeed the air could be painted blue, on the occasion when a golf ball they hit took a strange or bad hop. We all have seen clubs slammed into the ground.

I would like to point out here that through the years no one ever asks "Why me?" when a 60-foot putt rolls dead into the hole or a sand shot hits the flag stick and either falls stiff to the pin or falls into the hole, from a difficult lie in the aforementioned bunker. No one ever asked "Why me?" when that infamous hole in one occurs. We never seem to question a bounce off of a fence post and back in bounds again and the safety of the non-penalty area of the golf course. All of this happens because it is human nature to take for granted the good fortune we have and always have a need to question the bad turn of events that occur in our lives. I am as guilty as anyone for I have also asked the same question myself when it seemed that I was getting an unusual number of bad breaks in a specific period of time and I mean through several rounds of golf. Then I came to realize that those breaks, many of them, come with the choice I have made to play this grand game. I could look back on my golf life or my life in general for that matter and never for one minute think that I have had more bad breaks than I have had good ones. That would be ridiculous to the point of being ludicrous.

I have learned to approach the breaks in this game as I approach the breaks in my life. I still ask the question "Why me?" but the answer is vastly different today than it was in years gone by. Now "Why me?" is simple for me to answer, because I truly believe and realize that I am fortunate to be playing this game and living this life. Why me? Because I am blessed in more ways than I can count and in every walk of my life, on and off of the golf course. If someone asks me on the golf course, "Why me?" I merely say to them, it is because they are fortunate enough to be playing this game rather than so many other things that could have befallen them.

If someone feels like everyone else is getting good breaks but them and they need to ask, "Why not me?" the answer is basically the same. If you are in a foursome and one of the other players seems to get a number of good breaks, some of which beat you on a hole you played without a flaw, your first response is to wonder why those kinds of things do not happen to you. Two of the diseases that affect most all golfers are short-term memory loss and selective memory. Many times we have a hard time recalling all of the good things that happen to us on the golf course and in life in general.

On the other hand it is quite easy for us to remember the bad things that seem to happen to us on the golf course. I am sure, to a point of certainty, that the good bounces have come everyone's way at sometime or another. It seems to me that they (the good and bad bounces) all even out over our lifetime. I am also sure that a study of those events would prove that theory to be true. I know that is the situation in my life. There are people who seem to be more fortunate than others, but in the long run unless we self-destruct the breaks will all even out. Many times the people who seem to be more fortunate than most others around them have put themselves in a position to need that luck to help them out of bad situations. When we view their good fortunes we must take into account that they, more times than not, need luck to make up for their lack of skill in certain areas. If a person bounces a ball off of a tree or some other object, it is because he hit the ball in a direction that was less than correct. I would not trade direction for luck. Still we are fortunate when we have some of both.

Golf can and will most likely drive us crazy if we try to keep up with the good breaks and the bad bounces. If we feel that this game is cheating us out of some of the good luck we deserve, then we need to examine just what we are putting into the game of golf and what we expect to get out of it. That goes for life as well as golf.

Sadly golf can drive best friends apart. It can cause giant cracks and crevices in relationships that before seemed to be unshakable. The way we feel about golf and the good and bad breaks we get, often is the way we approach most of the things in our lives. In golf there are so many good things that happen to us and they somehow fade from our memory, as if they were just supposed to happen. Still we never forget the bad things in life that happen to us and all of those ugly bounces that took the spark out of our round on a particular day. We never want to take the credit for a bad break ourselves, never taking into consideration that what happened did so because of the wrong choice of clubs, the placement of our hands on that club, the swing plane and pattern, and so many other things of our own doing. Any of those elements or all of those items could have had a great deal to do with how the ball bounced or how the break happened or whether the ball faded or hooked into trouble. Many times the bad breaks are merely bad choices on our part rather than just bad luck. I am sure most balls that bounce out of bounds were hit in that direction. That may not always be the case, but it is safe to assume that is generally the situation.

Life is the same way for many people. They break their leg snow skiing and they feel cheated, without stopping for one minute to realize that they are so fortunate to be able to do something that only a fraction of the people in the world can afford to do. Other people feel cheated that their fathers died at the age of sixty-five or so and they never take the time to realize that many people in the world never even knew their fathers. It is hard sometimes to look beyond our own situation into what is really around us. If we did take the time to take that look we would realize just how fortunate we are to play a sport where we can get a bad break along with many good ones. Yet the major key here is that we are able to play this sport, at some level or another. That is starting with a good break.

We who are fortunate enough to play this game of golf have so many different reasons for loving it. For many of us it has become like part of our family merely because it has been in our lives for so long. It is for many of us an extension of ourselves. Many people have had golf in their lives longer than they have had certain members of their family in their lives, such as their children or their spouses. The relationship should be mature enough, in years, to be a binding one, on whatever level it abides, because it has stood the infamous test of time. I say whatever level, because it can cause us grief and it can grant us joy, and whatever emotions there are in between those two levels. As I have mentioned already several times, in life we sometimes re-member the bad things and take the good things for granted. Even though in golf we do the same thing, it seems that we tend to remember and replay many of the good shots and good times we have enjoyed with our friends. Human nature does allow us to remember the good times if not always the good bounces. In that way, this game of golf is no different from the game of life. A great example of human nature is to think about the person who wins the lottery and then complains that he or she has to pay taxes on the money they won. They focus on the negative in the wake of a waterfall of money.

It is true that golf brings into our lives both joy and frustra-tion, and for many people it has for a number of years. The game of golf should grant us peace, as I have stated time and time again. If that is not the case then why play it? I was reminded just the other day of two situations, relative to golf, that did occur in San Francisco. The first I happened to witness on the Golden Gate Bridge, late one summer afternoon as I was driving home from work. The driver in front of me stopped at the mid-span of the bridge and quickly got out of his car and went to the rear of the automobile. At first I thought he was going to jump off of the bridge, as so many people have done there through the years. Instead he opened the trunk of his blue Lincoln and removed his golf clubs, bag and all. He walked to the edge of the bridge and without even a hesitation, he heaved the golf clubs over the edge of the bridge and into the cold waters of the bay.

The people who were backed up behind me, normally would really have been angry over this delay and blowing their car horns. Instead they were laughing, and one man actually got out of his car and applauded the golf-clubless man, I guess for his strength and decision making. He may have been there himself at some point, who knows? I laughed about this incident most of the drive home, thinking just how addicted and/or attached we can get to this game and what we put ourselves through in the quest for perfection in it.

The following day in the newspaper was a story about a man in San Francisco who loved to play golf, according to his next door neighbor. One day the neighbor was looking out of his front window and he noticed that his golf-playing neighbor had parked his car, not in front of his own house, but rather in front of the neighbor's house who just happened to be observing this unfolding story from the front window of his home. He got out of his car, walked to the trunk of the car, opened it, and removed his golf clubs. He then walked to the curb area in front of his own house and placed each of the clubs precisely, with the heads of the clubs in the street and the grips of the clubs on the curb. He went directly back to his car, got into the car and drove right over the golf clubs, breaking every one of them in half. I believe it is safe to assume that neither of these former golfers had mental peace, as it related to this game and the search for perfection in it.

These two stories happened within two days of each other and they show us just how we can be tormented by something so wonderful, if we allow that to happen. You see for most people who play this game, peace is granted on some level, but it is not always acknowledged as such or controlled. There are days of frustration and there are days of sheer magic, no matter on what level one might play this game. The days of frustration can truly drive us crazy, because we do not really and truly understand our limits and/or our capabilities. A person who is playing this game might be doing the best they can possibly do, given their mental and physical talents. Then when they do not improve, frustration often becomes a major factor for them.

Truth in many situations is hard to deal with. I have played golf with people who get so frustrated at times I encourage them to quit playing golf for a while and try doing something else. It is hard to stop playing golf once you fall in love with it. Still we can learn from our frustrations and we can learn to accept imperfection. (I know that accepting is not always liking.) When we learn about accepting and frustration, we have learned a great lesson in the game of golf and the game of life. When this happens the understanding of imperfection gives both life and golf a powerful, new side and level.

This game of golf can give to us many gifts and one of those gifts is love. The same emotions we receive from family members and dear friends, we can receive from this wonderful sport. It is sad to come to grips with, but the relationship that some people have with golf last a great deal longer than other relationships in their lives. Those who were so close, for so long, fade away. This is brought about by either dying or those who were close to us just going away. Yet in our hearts they may still be a part of us, but golf remains with us until our physical bodies decide we can no longer go on in this quest for perfection. (One would hope that time would not occur until death.)

However if it does occur before death then our minds must take over and help us to remember all of the times in our lives when golf made us feel so special, because of place, time, and friends with which we shared many of those memories. Times when you heard the cheers of an adoring gallery as you walked along the golf course realizing that you were not alone, but indeed you were. We all can recall a special match in our minds when all we had to do was to sink a putt on the 18 hole to force a playoff with the likes of Palmer, Watson, Couples, Duval, or Mickelson. You will constantly remember all of the times you had to play just one more hole before it got dark and you could no longer see the hole at which you were putting. You can recall the one more trip you needed to take around the putting green before you had to leave or be late for supper or the times you were indeed late for supper.

You might remember, as I do, some of the times when tears came to your eyes and slid gently down your cheeks causing a warm feeling to pass through your heart, as you watched some golf champion on television say how grateful he was to God for the chance to be there, playing that game of golf and having those strokes of good fortune in his life—as Paine Stewart did after winning the 1999 U.S. Open Championship in Pinehurst. You feel somehow strangely akin to him because you also feel grateful to be able to play this game. I know that I do. If you have not felt that emotional surge in your relationship with golf, then you have barely begun your trek through the wonderful world of golf. If you could sit in front of your television set and watch Arnold Palmer walking up the 18 fairway in his final PGA Championship—with tears pouring down his cheeks because he knew in his heart that this was his last PGA Championship—and not feel those tears in your own soul, then your journey has yet to begin.

If you still need to ask, "Why me?" it is because you are fortunate to have the chance to be apart of the greatest of games going. I honestly feel that it would have been unfortunate for me if I had never played this game. Wow! What I would have missed. Yet the reality is, I did not miss the chance and because of that I am most fortunate. I could have died in that jungle in Southeast Asia, but I survived with the help of God and many people, to live another day and to play another round of golf.

Why me? Do you really have to ask? Why me? Because, I among all men am truly blessed…

> *We make choices in our lives.*
> *Some of them are good and some are not.*
> *Each day our innocence, arrogance, and wisdom*
> *Are put on display by our choices.*
> *Yet what really matters most are not our choices*
> *But rather the gifts we have been given,*
> *And whether we truly understand their roots*
> *And how we use them.*

CHAPTER NINE

The Bing Crosby Pro-Am (The Clambake)

There has been a great deal written in the past years about the mystical aspects of the game of golf. There are illusions of some strange shots and events that seem to be luck at first glance, yet somehow those events quite often seem to have a far deeper sense of purpose than just mere luck. I guess I believe that those shots, and others like them, are predestined to have a positive outcome even before they are struck. If this sounds to you as if I have just gotten a free ride on the insanity train, please bare with me for a few moments and I will share with you some personal experiences on the subject. These experiences have caused me to believe there is a specialness about certain times in our lives that is almost unexplainable. I say our lives because we are all capable of receiving these special times in our lives, if we are open to allowing them to come into our lives and if we are able to recognize them when and if they do.

Jack Nicklaus supposedly said that sometimes he sees some of his shots even before he swings at them or hits them. I know that he is referring to visualizing his shots. I also realize he is not a mystic, nor is he literally a Golden Bear. What it does show those of us who sit, watch, and wait is that special things can happen in our lives if we open our minds and hearts up to them and allow them into our game and into our lives. Someone once said, "If you expect a miracle that might be hard to find, but if you are open for anything, that could happen easily." It is a matter of being able to be patient and open at the same time, understanding we cannot always just pick our spots. (More times than not that is the case.)

In 1972 I was invited to participate in the Bing Crosby Clambake at Pebble Beach. Talk about miracles! But I was open for that to happen and it did. I did not see it coming, as Jack Nicklaus so often sees those wonderful shots of his, before he hits them. I was sitting in my office at the Letterman Army Medical Center in San Francisco, since I was still in the military at the time that special telephone call came. My secretary buzzed me and told me I had a phone call on line 2336. When I picked up the receiver the voice on the other end of the line said, "Chaplain Cherry, this is Bing Crosby and I would like to invite you to play in the Pebble Beach Pro-Am." My response was direct, "Right, who is this really?" feeling a bit like Bill Cosby in his comedy routine titled "Noah's Ark." I continued, "If you are really Bing Crosby you should say this is Bing Crosby and I would like to invite you to my tournament. Mmm-bo-ba-ba-boo." I was thinking that one of my friends was playing a practical joke on me, probably in retaliation.

There was a short span of silence and a bit of a soft laugh on the other end of the phone line and then the caller continued, "Chaplain Cherry, this is Bing Crosby and I would like to invite you to my golf tournament, Mmm-bo-ba-ba-boo." Of course I was in shock, because I realized at that point that it was indeed Bing Crosby himself who was talking to me. Still I was not enough in shock to keep me from accepting his more than gracious invitation. I was so excited about the chance to play with the big boys again, but also I was delighted at the prospect of playing golf at Pebble Beach, Spyglass, and of course the wonderful Cypress Point Golf Club. Simply put, this was a great chance to be in great golfer company and play on some really great golf courses.

At that time I was still a rather new amputee and my leg was still getting blisters on it from a poor fitting artificial limb. I knew that I was most likely going to have a difficult time walking in the event, but at that point I did not care. Blisters or no blisters I was going to play in "the Crosby."

As luck or something would have it, about two weeks before the beginning of the tournament I developed a genuine and grand case of the dreaded shanks. For those of you reading this, if you have never had a real case of the shanks, your golf education is woefully lacking in a big, big way. I was shanking everything from a 3 wood to my pitching wedge. I reached out to my local golf professional at the Presidio Golf Club for help. As he stood there watching me hit shank after shank, he could only shake his head in wonderment and amazement. I would hit bucket after bucket of golf balls and they all went dead right. I made certain that I was on the far end of the practice area, so I would not hit anyone to my immediate right. That is just how bad it was. I could just visualize me doing this time and time again at the Clambake.

"This is not what Jack Nicklaus visualizes," I said to myself. In pure disgust I put my clubs away and literally went back to the drawing board. I asked myself: "What makes a shank happen?" I finally figured it out, with a great deal of help from every golf book I could find in my house, a drawing pad, and mentally eliminating that strange fear of hitting the ball sideways. I knew that the fear of hitting the golf ball sideways would only go away with confidence inside of me that I could hit it straight once again. It happened. I finally felt as if I could go out and play golf again with mental peace—and only two days before my trip to the Crosby. I was ready for the 1st tee at the Clambake. Away I went to Pebble Beach with clubs and crutches in hand, literally. It was to be another gift of golf and gift of life for me.

When I arrived at the Fort Ord Officers Quarters, where I had arranged sleeping accommodations for the week, I felt very much at home merely because I was going from one army base to another army base. Yet there is where the feelings of comfort and being at home ended, at least for a short while. When I walked into Pebble Beach Golf Club to register for the tournament there were people from all walks of life milling around, and especially people from show business.

I eventually met the young professional who was to be with me for the duration of the tournament. His name was Paul and this was also his first Crosby. He was a stocky young man from New England, who could just hit the golf ball out of sight. A nice fellow and I often wondered to myself which of us was the most excited about playing in the Clambake. I was amazed at his swing and the distance of his drives, but I was to learn that he was like all of the other professionals there: it was their job and they were all good at it, relative to my game and the game of most of the amateur players there. The same is true as they relate to my profession, I have come to learn through the years.

The first day of the tournament our foursome played on the famous and private Cypress Golf Club. It reminded me just a bit of the Augusta National, I guess because it was so beautifully kept. There were deer roaming all over the golf course and as we approached the 15 green that beautiful day I could see the waves crashing against the ancient rocks that line the Pacific Ocean. It was truly a breathtaking sight to me at that time and it still is when I am fortunate enough to be in that area and play on any of those wonderful golf courses. John Dryden once said, "Art may err, but Nature cannot miss."

That is exactly the way I felt when I first saw that peninsula. It seems that golf, mankind, and nature have found such a delightful way to be joined at that spot, on this planet, for humanity's pleasure. Through the first 15 holes I did not play well; maybe I was distracted by the beauty around me or I could have been just playing poorly. As we crossed the street and headed to the 16th hole I realized we were approaching one of the most beautiful golf holes I had ever seen, to that point in my life. I was in awe of the giant crevice, over which the ball must carry to arrive safely from the tee onto the green. The shot was at least 190 yards, which looked more like a mile to me, as I stood there on the teebox. I watched as Paul hit his tee shot from the professional tees onto the green. The other two players in the group had already hit their shots unsafely into the cold Pacific Ocean. I took out my 3 wood and steadied myself and I hit the shot of my life, at least to that point. The ball landed on the front edge on the green, barely over a deep dive into a watery grave. It then rolled to a nice little spot about 20 feet from the flagstick. With help from my caddie, Gary, I lined the putt up and after much thought I struck the ball. The ball rolled slowly down the slight slope, turned ever so slightly to the right and dropped gingerly into the hole for a birdie two. It was merely a time for me to remember yet another blessing in my golf life.

Unbeknownst to me a photographer had captured both my tee shot over the water and the birdie putt as it was falling into the hole. To this day those two photos hang in my study as a reminder that all things are possible, even those shots that seem to be impossible or at least difficult at first glance. I also like to look at those photographs occasionally to remind myself that clothes fashions have really changed through the years. I no longer wear flower-patterned pants and wide leather belts. That day is a wonderful memory in a giant storehouse of memories for me, relative to this great game. The clothes are another story altogether.

My second day of golf in the Crosby we played the golf course at Pebble Beach. The weather was unusually beautiful. I say unusual because some of the Crosby's tournament weeks in the past had been accompanied by cold wind and/or rain. As a matter of fact the tournament in 1998 was postponed for about seven months because of the bad weather, after only 54 holes were played. The final round was played later that year in the summer months. In 1999 the tournament was shortened to 54 holes because of the extremely severe weather.

I was standing on the practice green putting when two men approached me. It was only ten o'clock in the morning and they were already well on the way to being inebriated. I was to find out later they were not getting drunk, they were still drunk from the parties they had attended the night before. They sort of walked over to me, as I was practicing my putting stroke, from about 5 feet. Anyone who has played golf with me knows that I am not a great putter by any stretch of the imagination. Still from 5 feet and on the same line time and time again anyone should be able to make those putts, even me.

The larger and older of the two men said, "I will bet you 5 dollars you cannot make that putt." I shook my head and knocked the putt straight into the hole, then I held my hand out for the reward, as much as a jocular gesture as anything else. After this scenario repeated itself several times and I was twenty dollars richer, he asked me if I was a professional golfer. Of course I realized at that point that he did not know much about golf. I have since learned that you should not try to judge any book by its cover and that is especially true in this sport. When he found out that I was not a professional golfer he wanted to know just how I got to play in the Clambake. I informed him that I had won the National Amputee Golf Championship and because of that victory I was invited to play in the tournament. He evidently thought that I had said the National Amateur Golf Championship, because when he asked where the tournament had been played and I told him he attempted to correct me by saying that the National Amateur had been played somewhere else other than where I had said.

I explained to him that the tournament was the National Amputee and not the Amateur. He looked rather puzzled and turned to his short friend, who had been more or less quiet through most of this encounter of a strange kind. The smaller man said, "He is missing something." I realized that I was smiling as they both looked down at my legs and I softly tapped on my left leg with my putter. The larger man just shook his head and walked away and no more words were spoken. I did notice the larger man a bit later on the 2nd hole peering through the sea of people. He was watching carefully what I was doing and how I was doing it. He and his friend were still smiling and still feeling pretty good, of that I was sure. They had sure made a great day just a bit better for me, by at least twenty dollars and probably even more.

The third day of the tournament I woke to the sound of a strong wind whistling through the trees just outside of my bedroom. As I got out of bed and peered out of the window I knew it was going to be a long and uncomfortable day at Spyglass Hills. I was not wrong. When Gary and I reached the practice range Paul was already there with his caddie and he, of course, was hitting practice balls. He was bundled up like he was going to play in the Alaskan Open rather than the Clambake. It was only a short time before I had also put on another layer of warm clothes to protect myself from the cold wind. We all knew that in the past two days we had been fortunate with weather. I had also been fortunate, as far as the blisters on my leg were concerned. They were not growing and that was indeed good news. That day the weather was not conducive to golf, but it was good for walking on an artificial leg. There was no heat to be found anywhere on the 18 holes of Spyglass Hills.

The wind was really blowing and right into our faces as we started play on the 1st hole. The hole is a par 5 and the wind usually comes right off of the ocean and up the 1st fairway, straight into the faces of the players coming off of that 1st tee. That day was no exception. The 2nd and 3rd holes were all right because one was a cross windhole, with some protection from the wind, because of the trees that line the right side of the fairway, while the other is a rather short and downhill par 3 hole. What made the short par 3/3rd hole a bit tough was the fact that we had to hit the golf ball right into the teeth of the wind. The 4th hole is a nice hole on a nice day, but that day was not a nice day, especially for golf. As we hit our tee shots the wind seemed to push our balls far to the right. On a normal day a second shot would have required no more than a 6 or 7 iron with a good tee shot. This by no means was a normal day, compared to the other days when I had played at Spyglass in the past. I took the 4 wood from my golf bag, after talking it over with Gary, who was already so cold, he could not have cared less about which club I hit. I looked at him and said, "Just think after this hole we only have 14 more holes to play." All I received from him for that piece of enlightened wisdom was a half smile and half a growl. He had a long list of other places where he would rather have been at that minute. I took a practice swing to see if the wind would bother my stance or just literally blow me over. When I got settled and finally hit the shot it turned ever so slightly into the wind and headed into the narrow valley that guards the front to the narrow 4th green. I felt that it was a good shot. It was then that I heard the gallery erupt. Paul said, "I think it went in. That is an in-the-hole crowd roar."

I looked at him and without excitement said, "I believe it did." I felt as it came off of the clubface, that it was going to go into the hole or at the least, it was going to be close to the hole. I actually felt that I saw the shot before it had happened. Unlike Nicklaus, I do not have that happen to me often, but that time it did. As I walked onto the green the hearty gallery gathered around there, applauded. I felt privileged to have been at that place and at that time. Another gift.

Many years later when I first heard Jack Nicklaus say that he saw shots before they ever really happened, I had just a bit of an inkling as to what he meant by that. I would never put myself in the same space with players like Nicklaus, but this game allows us all our own special space, our own special pleasures and moments, where we can function and have our own special joys. I am not invoking the metaphysical here, but there are questions of reality, response, and logic that need to be addressed at some point in our golf lives. As I walked to the back of the green on that cold morning someone who was warmly inside of a large yellow rain suit cried out to me, "It's in the hole." As I waved a thank you to him, I knew somewhere in the recesses of my mind, at the onset of the shot, as it was struck, that it was going to end up in the hole.

As I stood there on the back of the green waiting for the others to play out and watching the people in all of their brightly colored rain suits, I realized the ball I had hit landed on the top of the green and rolled all the way back to the hole and upon reaching the hole it fell straight into the bottom of the cup. I thought what a great game this is and how fortunate I was to be there—yes, in that nearly freezing rain and wind, enjoying that bit of the good life. Some people call those kind of shots lucky and I guess in a way they might be, but so are we all who can play this great game. I believe a 180-yard shot into a strong cross wind that finds the cup, has to be guided in some fashion or another, be that force divine, self-willed, or good fortune. The great part in all of this is we never know when that kind of thing will happen to us. We have to be open for that kind of experience to come into our lives.

There indeed might be someone watching over what we do. There are times, above and beyond the casual round of golf, when strange and wonderful things can and do happen. They probably happen more times than we realize because we are not thinking they could happen and we may not even be aware of them happening to us when they do. They may have happened already and we just did not realize that they happened, or recognize them for what they were. When the time is ripe and the situation presents itself, when something special happens, all I can say normally is, "Thank you, and I love this game."

I met Mr. Crosby himself at the Crosby Clambake that year, plus many other people, nice and otherwise. Yet, as I think about the parties I attended and the so-called special people whom I met, I do not remember much about them, because the time there was not about them, rather it was about golf. I remember some faces, but all of the other parts of that time seem a bit foggy in my memory. I will always remember the birdie I made on the 16th hole at Cypress Point and the eagle which happened to go in on the 4th hole at Spyglass Hills. I guess in reflective hindsight, of all I still remember that now seems important, I recall a loud voice coming from the gallery surrounding the 18 green as I walked onto it at Pebble Beach on the final day of the tournament. As I reached down to mark my golf ball, that voice like a foghorn on the bay in San Francisco, bellowed out of the otherwise solemn and quiet gallery. "Corbin Cherry, what in the hell are you doing out there?" To say the least I was startled until I realized that the voice came from an army officer, who at that time was stationed at Fort Ord. He had been in Vietnam with me. A warm and happy reunion took place on the fringe of the 18ᵗʰ green of one of the most beautiful golf courses in the entire world, as two grown men embraced—a reunion that was enjoyed by the entire gallery surrounding most of that green. If anyone wonders why I love this game, there are too many reasons for me to start counting all of them now.

> *If you walk along the ocean shore,*
> *Remember the shore itself may be void of virginity.*
> *But those feelings and thoughts that crash across*
>   *your soul and mind,*
> *Like the ocean waves over those ancient rocks,*
> *May well be a first and as pure as the spray from*
>   *a new wave.*

CHAPTER TEN

Holes in One (And Other Special Shots)

To ask anyone if they remember the first hole in one they made would be both presumptuous and even borderline unkind. First of all, most golfers have never had a hole in one, nor will they ever have one to remember in their entire life. Secondly, I doubt that anyone, in his or her right mind, could forget their first hole in one or any hole in one at all, for that matter. Still there are other shots besides the famous holes in one such as eagles and double eagles that do happen in people's golf lives, which in truth are many times harder shots than some holes in one might be. Those shots get far less notoriety and praise than any hole in one does. I have only seen one double eagle in my life and it was of course a 2 on a par 5 hole and it was a far better shot than any of the holes in one I have ever seen, except maybe two. The knowledgeable golfer will always remember from golf history the double eagle that Gene Sarazen made at the Augusta National, during the early years of the Masters Championship. Most people, myself included, do not know if Gene Sarazen ever even had a hole in one in his entire life, but he certainly did make that famous double eagle on the 15 hole at the Augusta National in 1935 and went on to win the Masters Championship. The shot that awarded him the 2 on the par 5 hole was a far greater shot than any ace he might have made on that same day, on any of the par 3 holes on that golf course.

About two years ago I happened to be watching a PGA tournament on television and one of the most successful golfers of our time made a hole in one. That player's shot was covered by the television cameras all the way from the striking of the ball off of the tee until it rolled right into the hole. I was surprised and yet not so, to hear the announcer say that it was, for this prominent golfer, his first hole in one ever. Yet that is the nature of these special shots. Some people seem to make a great number of aces, while others never taste that oh so sweet nectar.

Not everyone is granted that special gift and joy. The truth is we never know just what is around the corner for us in this game. Today what seems like strokes of bad luck turn into rays of good luck tomorrow or as was stated earlier, even on the next hole or the next shot. That is still another reason why we play this mentally joyous and frustrating game. The idea of making an eagle or a double eagle, though they are much harder sometimes to pull off than a hole in one, just does not sound as good as making a hole in one does. Still many people believe that an ace is possible and maybe we think that a double eagle might not be.

The first hole in one I ever witnessed was made by a 24 handicapper. I am sure he most probably wet his pants when the golf ball he hit rolled right into the hole, though I do not know that for sure. He certainly was excited, as he should have been. He acted as if that was exactly what he was trying to do. The situation occurred in a Pro-Am event in North Carolina. Our team was made up of one professional and three amateurs. I have often wondered how the professionals deal, mentally, with playing in all of the Pro-Ams that come their way. The amateurs handicaps ranged from 7 to the aforementioned 24. The professional in our group was a longtime touring pro whose first name was Fred. I was a 7 handicap at the that time and there was another amateur in the group whose family name was also Cherry (no kin of mine), who was a 10-handicap player. The 24 handicapper was a sportscaster for one of the local television stations.

Even now, all of these years later, I recall the situation so vividly, because it was our 10th hole and the sports announcer had not even finished one hole in the first nine we had previously played. He had literally picked his ball up on every hole we had played to that point, merely because he could not help the team on those holes. When his turn came to swing at the ball on the 10th hole, and I use the term swing loosely, he hit a mighty shot with his 4 wood. The ball traveled 180 yards, as straight as an arrow toward the flagstick.

It hit right on the front part of the green and as if it had radar, then rolled right toward and dove into the cup. A hole in one. The expression on his face was priceless. He was in total awe of what had just happened to him. That is and again I will say it, what this game can do for us and to us if we are open for those things to happen. I must add here that with all of the screaming, celebrating, and hand-slapping that went on, his hole in one was the last hole he finished in that round—but who cared? Not anyone in our group, of that I am sure. I was happy for him and secretly I wondered if my turn would ever come someday. Somehow I never worried about it, because those things will happen when the time is right.

I have already mentioned in the prior pages that I have had enough joy as it relates to golf and other dimensions of life, to fill the lives of a hundred people or more. This is certainly true as it relates to golf shots in particular. At the time of these musings I have had the honor of being the recipient of 15 holes in one. I am sure that is more than my share, but I am still looking for more, if they come my way. I am not greedy, but they are out there, just waiting for us all.

My first hole in one came after many years of watching golf balls I hit, roll up to the hole and hit the flagstick and bounce away. Like so many other people I have had to repair the surface around the cup, from near misses, in attempts to get that first elusive ace. I had seen so many of my golf shots just refuse to go into the hole, as if the hole had a cellophane cover over it. Strangely enough I never felt frustrated about those streaks of what could be considered bad luck, because they were good shots that just never found the bottom of the cup. I was happy to have hit a good shot and I was just feeling so fortunate to be playing the game of golf. I always tried to be reasonable about how the shot was hit and the distance the ball travels, the size of the cup with the flagstick in it. I always knew that it would take a perfect shot to allow a golf ball of 1.68 inches to slide in between the edge of the cup and the flagstick. There seems to be hardly any room for the ball to get into the hole to begin with, yet sometimes it happens.

Warm and wonderful things happen in the game of golf and the game of life.

The dawn of my holes in one came when I was playing golf in New Jersey with a friend I had met at Walter Reed Army Medical Center, during my rehabilitation after Vietnam. He was also an amputee as a result of the war over there. We were playing the par 3/8th hole on his home course. My friend had hit his tee shot onto the green, but left of the pin. The green was actually partially obscured by the elevation of the terrain. I hit a 3 iron straight in the direction of the flagstick. As the ball sailed toward the green, the caddie who was standing up on the right side of the green, watched the golf ball as it flew by him. He watched the shot and then he turned toward our foursome and held up one finger. There was a moment of silence and then I knew what it felt like to have a hole in one.

My friend said, "You made an ace!" I smiled and tried to act as if it was just another day's walk in the park, but inside I was churning like a cheap watch or an old Lincoln on the interstate. I never mentioned the hole in one again for the rest of the round or after it, even though people were congratulating me left and right. Of course, as is the custom, everyone wanted their free drink. (The person making the hole in one buys everyone present a drink.) I never have been able to come to grips with the reasoning behind hitting a good shot and being penalized to the tune of two hundred dollars or more. Everyone in the clubhouse seemed surprised that I was so calm. I maintained a calm exterior throughout the hour or so after the round was completed. I soon investigated and found out about hole-in-one insurance.

Sometime later that day when we were leaving the golf course and heading to my friend's home for dinner, I recall asking him to roll up all of the windows in the car and cover his ears, so I could just scream and get it over with. I did just that and it seemed to be over. The whole affair affected me rather strangely. Once it was over, it was over. The rush of the shot was over maybe until the next time. When I recall that first hole in one, it makes me happy, but the shot I hit on the 4th hole at Spyglass in the strong wind during the Crosby tournament, was a far better shot, be it luck or otherwise.

People say that holes in one are luck and many of them are indeed just that, but my theory is that if you hit the ball at a target and the ball finds the target, then it certainly should not be considered merely luck. That is where you were aiming. Art Wall, who during his professional career, won a number of tournaments on the PGA Tour, was reputed to have made more holes in one than anyone else in professional golf. I saw him make an ace in the latter part of his career in a celebrity golf tournament. He was being interviewed following that particular round of golf and he said, "I have never figured out why there is so much excitement about a hole in one. I merely hit the ball at the target and it went in. After all that is where I was aiming." I have a golfing friend in Southern California whose name is Bill and he refers to one's direction, as their "Towards." I truly believe that if your "Towards" is good, good things will happen in your golf game and in life itself. They certainly have a way of running side by side.

After that day in New Jersey and that first ace, the gates opened up wide for me and I had 2 more holes in one in the next three weeks. I made one in Southern California in the warm sunshine and I had another one in the pouring and cold rain in Canada one week later. Both of those shots, be they skill or luck, were made in tournaments. Yet neither one of those aces netted me an automobile. I have seen quite a number of holes in one in my life, but I have never seen one that resulted in someone winning a new car. Although I do know a man who had 2 holes in one in three months and he received an automobile for each of them. Timing is everything, in golf and in life.

I once made a hole in one in a tournament and on my own birthday. Now that is a nice birthday present. It was especially nice since my former wife had forgotten that it was my birthday altogether. By the way that is not the reason she is my former wife.

Driving home from the tournament that day, I was thinking that a man could ask for no more than to make a hole in one on his birthday. Good thing too, right?

Once while playing on my home course with the then president of our golf club, I mentioned to him when we reached the par 3/4th hole that I had picked up a new club two days before, just for that particular hole. Now that par 3 hole is 175 yards from the back tees to the center of the green. The wind is almost always in your face as you stand on the tee. The ball must carry all the way to the green or else it will roll all the way back down into the valley, which will result in a not so easy flop shot back up onto the green. I had never even hit that new club before that day, and after telling David this, I confidently approached my tee shot. The wind was doing its usual thing and the sky was its normal gray self. When I hit the golf ball it started right at the flagstick. It stayed precisely on line and it flew right into the hole. When our foursome walked onto the green, the only conversation I heard from my playing partners was that the shot was not a greenie, because it was under the green and not on the green.

We were playing greenies, sandies, birdies, and all of the other fowl of the golfing world. Of course, they did not win that argument. The first shot with the club and it found a home in the hole.

The following year I was playing again with the same gentlemen and when we reached the 16th hole I remarked that it was December 29 and I had not had a hole in one in that calendar year. The 16th hole is a long par 3, more than 200 yards from tee to green. The green is surrounded by bunkers and it has a small opening at the front of the green as an entrance way onto the green. The pin was tucked on the right side of the green behind a bunker. I took out my 3 wood and hit a shot that seemed to work its way around the bunker, then bounced a couple of times and rolled smoothly right into the hole.

David looked at me and said, "This is getting spooky!" Actually it felt a bit spooky—in a good way. It felt as if something was going on for which I had no answer or control, but I liked it. I remembered hearing people talk about Babe Ruth pointing to the outfield when he approached home plate and then hitting the ball over that particular part of the fence, be it truth or fiction. I sort of felt that way, just a bit.

I have often told my friends that sometimes I feel as if a hole in one is coming on, because of the nature of the shots I've been hitting and the direction of flight the ball seems to have at certain times. It is almost as if one of the shots has to go into the hole because they are coming closer and closer to doing so. There is something special in this game many of us do not take the time to search for. There are many special events that occur in both golf and life and we should feel privileged when we are on the receiving end of them. Another reason there is an answer to the question, "Why me?" Because you and I are most fortunate.

I do have a plan to go somewhere special with the idea of holes in one. I do not intend to just talk about my own aces. Yet these shots are so unique to this game that we cannot talk about golf and not mentioned their significance. Each one is a story all its own. If someone makes a hole in one, it is theirs to keep for the rest of their lives. That makes the golfer who is the proud recipient of that hole in one, a special person and in a special and prominent category of golfers.

The same friend, that I mentioned earlier who talks about a person's "Towards" and lives in Southern California is an avid golfer himself and a fine player. As I mentioned earlier his name is Bill. On one occasion he was playing golf in Colorado and made a hole in one on the same hole that his favorite uncle had aced 28 years before. I am sure he was really thinking about his uncle when the ball rolled into the hole and his uncle was happy to be looking down on that shot. A hole in one that will forever be remembered by my friend who was rewarded for a good shot with excellent "Towards."

I want to insert here a bit of trivia and history about the often elusive hole in one. In 1964, a gentleman playing on what was then the Del Valle Country Club in California, made consecutive holes in one. Not only is this a remarkable feat and hard to believe, but they were made on the 7th and 8th holes of that golf course. One was a 336-yard par 4 and the other was a 290 yard par 4.

The longest straight hole in one ever recorded was made on a 447-yard hole, on the Miracle Hills Golf Club in Omaha, Nebraska. I would say that a miracle happened in 1965 at Miracle Hills.

Still the longest hole in one ever recorded occurred in 1995. The hole was a dogleg par 5 that bent around a large grove of trees. The hole is 496 yards. The shot was hit over the trees in an attempt to cut the dogleg. I guess the strategy paid off in the form of a one. This occurred in England, on the Teign Valley Golf Club. The player who hit the teeshot that found the hole that day, hit the shot over the trees while trying to cut the corner of the dogleg for a short second shot to the green, and he hit the golf ball where he intended. I said, "Good shot."

The oldest person to make a hole in one was 99 years young and he made the hole in one in 1985.

The youngest person to record a hole in one was five years of age and he made the hole in one in 1998.

There are so many different kinds of positive events that occur in the lives of so many golfers who hit certain and special shots. Those events are so special that they will never be forgotten, and that almost goes without saying, but I will say it anyway.

Were those shots luck or skill, or were they guided?

Who cares? What really matters is that they did happen!

Some years ago there was an elderly gentleman who belonged to our golf club. He had been an army chaplain during World War II. I think he loved golf almost as much as I did and sometimes that too was up for heated debate. Not long after I met Walter he was going through a time in his life of rather bad health. He was having a great deal of trouble breathing and that of course cut his golf life somewhat short. On many afternoons I would drive up into the parking lot of the golf club and see him sitting in his car, right behind the 18 green, smoking his pipe. He was watching the players come to the last hole and most likely eating his heart out that he could not be out there playing alongside them. There were times when I would go over to where he was sitting and get into the car and sit with him. We would talk about some of the people finishing up their round and of course we would critique many of their golf swings. He was a real student of the game of golf. I always believed he was more of a mental student than a physical student of this game.

As time would have it—and does for all of us in our lives at some point—I got a call one morning that Walter had passed away. That day his wife informed me that he had wanted his ashes strewn somewhere on the golf course. When I approached the manager of the golf club with a request to place Walter's ashes somewhere on the golf course, he informed me that such a thing was forbidden. He paused. Then he said, "You do know of course that the golf course is closed on Mondays."

I took the hint and on the following Monday, Walter's widow and I found our way to a nice green spot just behind the 6th green. A pretty little par 3 hole, with the teebox high above the green. The green is surrounded by bunkers and tall, beautiful trees. Together behind that green we laid Walter to rest. You might ask, "So what?" On the following Wednesday, a mere two days later, when I was playing that hole for the first time since we had spread Walter's ashes there, I stopped on the teebox and before hitting my tee shot I thought about Walter and how much he really did love the game of golf. When it came my turn to hit my shot the ball flew off of the clubface straight and true.

My "Towards" was good. The ball hit about 2 feet in front of the pin and dove right into the hole. When I reached the green I repaired the ball mark, gently retrieved the golf ball from the hole, walked to back of the green, and peered down to where

Walter's ashes lay. I just had to say, "Walter this one was for you," tipping my blue visor gently and discreetly to him.

When I called Walter's wife later that same day and told her about what had happened on the 6th hole she asked if I was surprised. I had to say no. What had happened was not a surprise at all to me and that it happened where it did and when it did, was also not a surprise. Strange and wonderful things happen in this game of golf and life when we are open for them to happen. Her closing comment to me was, "I am sure Walter is happy. So am I." That made three of us.

I will never be able to understand how someone can believe that this kind of visitation, in the form of golf shots, could be of the occult. The occult is too dark—the divine maybe, but not the occult. You see there are shots that are special because of time and place. They are also special because they happen to us. Holes in one and those other special shots are out there waiting for us to find them and make one of those special shots, our own.

> *The magic garden is where flowers grow*
> *From no seeds whatsoever,*
> *Save seeds of thought and suggestion.*
> *The magic garden is where time and matter*
> *Come face to face*
> *With what often seems to be a supernatural force.*

CHAPTER ELEVEN

Being With Friends (As Good As It Gets)

There are so many wonderful things, at least for me, about being involved with this game of golf and the game of life, which of course go hand in hand if that is our desire. Just take for instance the mere fact of being with people about whom you care and who care about you, on a stretch of wonderful green grass, on a warm spring or autumn day. For that matter any season of the year is a good time to be playing golf with one's friends. That to me is the epitome of joy.

Of course it is also possible that someone might be willing to spend time alone playing golf on that same beautiful patch of God's green earth. There is a deep specialness and joy about this time in one's life. It is true that it may be hard for some people to spend time alone, doing the things that make one feel alone, but that is not the case when it comes to golf, at least not for me. Still being with good and special friends on the golf course of our choice, is a special treat indeed. Being with those friends truly makes the package totally complete.

I was in Florida on one occasion to play a member guest golf tournament. After one of the rounds in the tournament, a rather large group of the competitors decided that we needed and wanted to play 9 more holes of golf. Away we went, all sixteen of us in twelve golf carts. It was truly like a madhouse of ready golf. When you got to your ball you hit it then, no questions asked. When I got to my ball, on that 1st hole, I had some of those same feeling I had experienced earlier on in my golfing life, when it was play as much as you can and as fast as you can. There were golf balls everywhere. It was truly a ready format of golf. Everyone was moving fast and hitting their shots whenever they reached their golf ball. We had a great time, but I am certain, had I seen this spectacle from afar and not been involved in it, I would have felt as if it were not the proper way to play this sport or the proper way to act in relationship to this sport. I am sure that both would have been the case to any outsiders who might have observed those weird goings on. Still we—all sixteen of us—were truly having fun and after all, that is the reason why we should play this game. I must admit it looked more like a run and shoot offense from the NFL than a golf outing. There were carts everywhere and people hitting shots from every direction. The good part, other than all of us playing golf together, was that we were all with friends. Not all good friends, but golfing friends. The other good part in this whole adventure was that no one got hit by a flying golf ball, Tit-lest, or otherwise.

There are people who I could name in these pages with whom I would play golf anytime and anyplace and under nearly any circumstances, because I love this game and I love them and I find true pleasure and real fulfillment in their company. From the sandhills of North Carolina, to Music City, USA, to the cornfields of Indiana, from the windy plains of Texas, to the deserts of Arizona and on to the Pacific Ocean coast of California. When I think of them as my friends and I think of golf, that is when I think about and realize true beauty, and something special comes into my mind and heart. When I think of the things that grant me peace of mind and all of the blessings that are mine, God-given most of them, I think of friends who have granted me a place in their lives. Part of that space and place has to do with golf and special times and places we shared. I will forever be indebted to golf for making this history happen in my life. The Pulitzer Prize–winning author Rene Dubos once wrote, "Man shapes himself through decisions that shape his environment." So we do when we choose our special games and our special friends and place both together in our environment.

Back in 1981 I was living in the northern part of Virginia and working in Washington, D.C. One beautiful late summer morning the heat had begun to subside and the early fall tones were coming into their own. I was happy because this day was going to be a golf day for me and I was anticipating the joy that most always accompanies such a time for me. What occurred on that day for my playing partner (friend) and myself, was a rapid fire 72 holes of fast golf.

Normally under no circumstances would I have attempted such a feat, merely because I thought I had outgrown such golf adventures. I could understand those numbers say in two days, but not in one single day. I must say in our defense that the deed was not done with outright forethought. It was about 7:30 in the morning and we had started out to play only 36 holes and those 2 rounds went by so fast and it seemed as if we just kept coming to the end of another round and there was still plenty of daylight left. There was absolutely no one else on the golf course, so on we went and on we went and on we went. We did it and it was a wonderful day of fellowship, laughter and golf. I am sure there were a number of shots we silently disliked and in some cases not so silently disliked, but we were playing golf and having fun. As I have said before and probably will say again, that should be the primary reason anyone plays this game in the first place.

All of this lasted until the young man from the golf shop came out in a golf cart to inform us that we had to come in and return the golf cart we were driving, so the employees could go home. I am sure that he was probably a bit miffed, but also a bit amused when we told him we had only one more hole left to play. At that point we were on the green of hole number 71. I watched as the young man from the pro shop drove away toward the 18th teebox, still a bit disgruntled, but I am certain that he was silently amused at the two older guys who wanted to play golf until dark or forever, whichever came first. Dick laughed as we headed up the 72nd fairway, after we convinced the young man that we would come right in after the next hole. He said, "I do not understand why we have to get the cart in so early, we still have at least fifteen minutes of daylight left." He was right, we could have played a few more holes, but the day was done and if we stayed out there any longer we might be burned at the stake by the employees still working in the golf cart barn and the pro shop. They wanted to go home, and rightly so. While we were having fun, they were working, far past overtime.

That is why this game is what it is and why it is the way it is. No other sport, to my knowledge, will allow you to be a part of it for twelve to fourteen hours and still want more. In those hours there was joy and agony, but there was peace and friendship. I guess all of those emotions are important. That is what this game brings to us. Yes it will bring us agony, but that will soon pass away, like a summer thunderstorm. Yet the joy and friendship that are ours because of golf will be with us for many years to come, like the beautiful sunsets that seem to go right down into the ocean, thousands of miles away.

We will rarely forget those special sunsets and those special times with our golfing friends.

Once, years before I was able to play golf well and really felt as comfortable as I do most of the time now, a friend—who feels more like a brother to me than a friend—and I decided that we would go from the eastern part of North Carolina, where we and our families lived, to the western part of the state to participate in a golf tournament. We drove nearly three hours to finally arrive at our destination in Statesville, North Carolina. We actually did well in the event and came home with a car full of trophies and golf merchandise. The format for the event was threefold, a best ball team, a low net prize, and a low gross individual prize. I do not really remember who won what, but I do remember that from that time to this day, a true and lasting bond was formed between Jack and myself. There will never be a chance to play golf with him again in my life, anywhere, that I will pass up. I remember one time in Texas while visiting with him and his family, we were scheduled to play golf. I woke up the morning of the golf match and felt so bad because of a brand-new case of the flu coming on. Did I stay in bed?

You know better. I did what I felt was more important. Most of the things in my life I would have passed on doing that day, but one of those was not playing golf with Jack. Did he get the flu? No because that was one thing I did not want to share with him. I recall once he and I were scheduled to play golf in the Austin area of Texas and Jack woke up with an incredible migraine headache. Did he still play golf on that day? You guess, because I already know the answer. This game truly has made us family. I have always felt that it is good to win a golf match, be it a tournament or a social match, but friendships in golf last a lot longer than the glitter of any trophies of victory, which unlike those warm memories will most assuredly tarnish in time.

As you read these words I am sure that each of you has a special friend or two, made that way through golf. It is nice when those friends last long past golf stories and other things of a material nature. Some of you may think you do not need golf friends, that you had rather be alone. If that is the case then I can honestly say you have not witnessed, firsthand, the true joy of fellowship that being with a friend can bring to anyone who might be open for that to happen to them. At my golf club in San Francisco, there is man who always plays golf by himself. I do not mind playing golf alone and I have played alone in many instances, but this man seems always to be so alone. I feel as if I would like to grab him and shout, "You need a friend!"

I asked him a couple of times to join a threesome in which I was playing and he just politely said, "no." I feel bad because he is missing so much, but the other side of the coin is, I am not. Maybe he likes his own company more than other people's company, with which he has played in the past.

Playing golf is one thing, but playing golf with people whom you love, makes golf the special thing it is. There are those who love golf and there are those who LOVE GOLF. There is something special about someone who really loves this game, not just for the scores, not just for the places that they are able to play, but because all of the above go together to allow them to just LOVE GOLF. This goes beyond winning and losing to only winning. When these particular people play golf they always win, no matter what they shoot or how they play. This does not mean they do not want to win or that they do not want to always shoot low scores. What it does mean is that they want to play golf. It means that they really LOVE GOLF.

There is a group of friends of mine who gather together once a year. Many people have such groups of friends in their lives, maybe, and if that is the case then I am happy for them. There are eight in the group and from time to time the group changes its faces and its names, but not its intent. The group started with the idea of two wonderful friends of mine, Jack, whom I mentioned earlier, and John from Tennessee. (Just to show you that we are open-minded within the group, John is a lawyer.) We gather together in the southeastern corner of North Carolina for the sole purpose of playing golf. That is exactly what we do for eight straight days. We play 36 holes of golf each day and on two different golf courses each day, weather permitting. So for 8 days we play 288 holes of golf on 16 golf courses. Everyone in the group cares about winning and losing. They care about their scores and they take pride in their games, but they are there because of the golf and the friendship that comes from being with the group. To talk to some of them you might think they are too smooth to be caught up in that kind of an emotional situation. They might seem too involved in their professions, as varied as those professions are, yet golf and the feelings of friendship that come with the game of golf, have a way of making those involved in them different somehow. Golf and the joy of fellowship with like-hearted people makes that trip to North Carolina happen every year.

While playing in a golf tournament in southern California one year, a friend of mine also playing in the tournament and I decided we would go to another golf course, close to the tournament venue, for another 18 holes of golf after the morning round at the tournament site was complete. We did this because the rules stated that we could not play golf on the same golf course where the tournament was being played, during the tournament. It has to do with practice. We got started a bit later than we had hoped to and by the time we reached the 16th hole it was getting rather dark. From the 17th tee we hit our shots into the darkness and in the direction of the lights on the club-house. I had done that before. As we arrived at where we thought our shots might have ended up and were fumbling around in the dark trying to find our golf balls, a young man came out in a golf cart to tell us we needed to bring the golf cart in at once, because it was dark. (Does that sound familiar?) I explained to the young man that Curtis and I were close to par and we needed only ten minutes to finish our round.

He smiled, as if he had been there before and said he would be right back and away he drove into the night. We had already hit our second shots to the 17th green or at least in that direction by the time he returned. When he arrived he was in a pickup truck with great large lights mounted on the top. We could see almost perfectly because of his help and imagination. We finished our round, a seventy-two and a seventy-four and a hearty tip for the truckster. We could have stopped, but not easily, because we only had a hole and a half to play. We both love this game so much so, we even play it in the dark, with or without a flashlight or a truck with huge lights. Of course daylight is better and with friends like Curtis, it is far better, day or night.

Some years ago I was playing golf for a week in Hawaii and I just happen to remember, that the course on which I was about to play, was the favorite golf course of one of my best golfing friends. He had told me about playing there before and how beautiful he thought that place was. He was certainly a hundred percent correct. As I was on the driving range hitting practice balls and anticipating what I knew would be a wonderful experience of playing golf there, I thought I should give my friend a call, especially since he was back in California and working so hard. I found a telephone just outside of the Pro Shop and placed a call to his office in San Francisco. When the secretary answered, I asked for him. When he came on the line I said, "Larry, guess where I am?"

He knew just exactly where I was and what I was about to enter into, because he had been there himself. As I walked down the 1st fairway and looked out at the great and beautiful Pacific Ocean, the whales were playing and dancing there, as if they were as happy as I was. I had shared with one of my friends some-place we both really loved and the medium that takes us there.

In one period of my life, there were quite a number of years that passed by in which I never saw my brother. The reasons for that visitational hiatus are not at all clear to me and truly unim-portant I guess to anyone other than my brother and myself. We had always lived far away from each other during those years and that could be one of the reasons for not seeing much of each other. When he was in the army I was not and when I was in the army, he was not. Many years ago we had been able to play golf once together and that did not happen again until I went to visit him in the spring of 1996.

My brother, whose name is Bill, had through the years de-veloped into a fine striker of the golf ball. His scores were certainly lower than they had been when first we played golf together, all those years before. After my visit, when I was leav-ing Augusta, where my brother and his family live, I thought about how nice it had been to spend time playing golf with my brother. It was a real joy to see him playing this game that I love so much and to be playing it so well. It was most of all gratifying to see him enjoying the game and not getting so bent out of shape and frustrated at the bad shots, which we all hit occasion-ally and sometimes even more often than that. I was happy to spend those days with my brother playing the only game we have ever been able to play together, for various reasons, and above all having fun doing it.

He once said to me, "I was so proud when I saw you playing in the U.S. Open!" I was touched to hear him say that and to know that he knew I had been there and done that. Yet more than anything else, I was glad to have played those three days of golf with my brother and to be able to talk with him and tell him I loved him. He needed to know I was proud of his golf game and happy to have been, through golf, allowed to spend that quality time with him. Golf, you did it again.

I have already said in these writings and more than a num-ber of times also in real life, that I prefer to play golf with people

I care for rather than people that I do not care for. Those people who are no fun to be around can make a bad day of golf even worse and they can spoil a good round and a special, beautiful day. That is simple logic. Yet that is a negative approach to something so positive. I could write down in these pages, without fear of argument, the names of a number of people with whom I could play golf every day for the rest of my life and never get tired of their company. It may well be that I am not on their list of favorites, but I believe I probably am, because feelings transcend verbiage. Still I could play golf with them anywhere because of who they are and how they are entangled in my life and of course, because of golf itself. The other reason I could play golf with them is because they love golf in the same universe of caring that I do.

Comradery in golf is only one of the real pleasures this great game allows us. We all love to score, to hit long drives, and to make those tricky putts. We all have played rounds of golf by ourselves and I assume that many people are like I am. I find those moments of solitude special, as I do the times that I spend playing golf with my friends. Some people I know do not like to play golf alone. I like it either way, with or without company. Still the right company makes it unbeatable.

I remember times when I have pulled for a friend to miss a putt, (I have to be honest), but I have never wished for a friend of mine to hit a ball out of bounds or into a lake, even down in the deepest and darkest recesses of my mind. That does not imply that I do not want to win or that I do not wish to beat my opponents, no matter who they are. Here I have to disagree with Vince Lombardi who said, "Winning isn't everything, it's the only thing!" To me it is important to win or I would not have this fire in my belly to play this wonderful game and to beat whomever I am playing against or whatever course I am fortunate enough to be playing on. I would prefer that each person, with whom I am playing, would play the best they can play and then let the chips fall where they may. Again this is a game and best played when you are with friends even though alone is also special. Friends are just another reason I love this game. We win at golf always when we play the game with friends, no matter whose score is the lowest on the scorecard.

I played the famous old golf course Burning Tree a while back I and was shown the following inscription, which was placed on a plaque in 1933 and attached to a large concrete water fountain named the Fountain of Health. This fountain is located on the 13th hole of this wonderful old golf course. The inscription reads as follows:

> *Water is the gift of the gods, tarry here for*
> *a moment*
> *And have a little drink with me.*
> *My everlasting wish for you*
> *Is good health and long life*
> *And pars and birdies in everything that*
> *you undertake.*

If you think the gentleman golfer who wrote the above passionate inscription did not truly and divinely love playing golf with his friends, then you have never had a real group of golfing friends. I, on the other hand, have and I thank God everyday for their sharing their lives with me. If I can borrow a bit of the above author's sentiment, "I wish all of them pars and birdies in all they undertake."

> *Today I stood and watched a parade pass by*
> *And I was the only one who witnessed it,*
> *Because it was deep and not so deep*
> *In the canyons of my own mind.*
> *My friends were all there*
> *Walking by, one by one.*
> *How fortunate I am because*
> *Not only did I find myself smiling,*
> *But they too were doing the same.*

— CHAPTER TWELVE —

One Night

It was 1986 and I was in Las Vegas, Nevada, to play a golf tournament. As usual I was excited about having a chance to play a new golf course and have an opportunity to meet some new people. The first three days of the tournament I played well—in fact well enough to find myself in first place after the first 3 rounds of the 72-hole tournament were completed. How I played is not the reason for the inclusion of this chapter in this book about golf, but it did have an impact on the reason for this chapter being written. The *Las Vegas Review-Journal*—I believe that is the correct title of the publication—was one of the local newspapers in the Las Vegas area at the time I played in the tournament. They had covered the event for the first three days and on the morning of the fourth day's play, one of the headlines in the sports section read: "Amputee Leads Golf Championship." I mention this here, not because I won the tournament or even because I had the lead in the tournament after 3 rounds, but rather because of what happened as a result of that headline being published in the newspaper and the story that accompanied the headline.

The story goes like this. As I walked off of the 18th green on the last day of the tournament, soaking wet from perspiration caused by the heat of the desert sun, several people greeted me. I signed my scorecard, shook hands with them, and received some verbal rewards for a job well done. I was happy to have won the golf tournament. I was headed for the clubhouse, a cool shower, and a cold drink, when I was approached by a slender woman in her late thirties. I was thinking she might be coming over to congratulate me, but the congratulations never really came.

Instead she said to me, "Corbin, it has been a long time." Now mind you I am good at remembering faces, but I was truly stumped about who this woman was. "You don't remember me, do you?" she asked. At that point I was slightly off of my game for the first time during that whole day. I had done well through the first 18 holes, but I was fading fast coming into the 19th. She continued, "Corbin it is okay if you do not remember me, because I have changed a great deal and it has been almost fifteen years." When Sarah told me who she was I remembered her vividly and was shocked, to say the least, by how much she had physically changed. When I knew her, she was a young and almost innocent looking woman with her dreams and ambitions out there in front of her. As we walked toward the clubhouse my mind surfed back to the time when I had first met her, all those many years before. I recalled that we had met on a flight from San Francisco to Tampa.

In the months after that we had corresponded and arranged to see each other on a trip I was taking to Miami. We had dinner one night and the next day she invited me to accompany her to see Elton John perform. Sarah was definitely correct, she had changed a great deal from her earlier days. It was not just her age, because she was still young in years and attractive in a maturing way. She just looked tired and almost used up.

As we sat at a table out under a canopy, there at the golf course, she told me a story that was truly hard for me to imagine, but one that sadly, I had heard too many times before in my life. She said she had almost lost her life in a relationship with drugs and alcohol. She mentioned she had abused life in almost every way possible. I looked out across that tranquil green grass covering the 18 fairway and I silently wished she had started playing golf instead of all of the other things she had been involved in, but I knew it was too late.

I wanted to change the conversation a bit so I asked Sarah how she knew I was there in Las Vegas. She told me she and some friends had come to Las Vegas for a weekend of shows and they had gone into a restaurant for breakfast early that morning. When they sat down at the table to eat, a newspaper was lying in their booth, with the sports page turned up. The headline read, "Amputee Leads Golf Tournament." It of course piqued her interest and she said she could not believe the name that jumped right out of the story. "I just wanted to talk to you so badly. I guess I needed to talk to you." That she did—through dinner, well into the wee hours of the morning, as we sat sometimes quietly in my hotel room. Finally she layed her head back on the big stuffed chair and fell asleep. I covered her up with a blanket and went to sleep myself, in a world of amazement.

When I awoke in the morning she was gone, but there was a note on the chair where she had slept, It read, "I will always be grateful to golf, because it introduced us all those many years ago, on your way to Tampa to play a golf tournament, and because in this particular instance your being here probably saved my life." That was it and that was enough for me. I sat down there in that same big stuffed chair where she had been sleeping and it was still alive with the scent of her perfume. I read the note over and over again, because the meaning went far deeper than morality. It went to the crust of the pie that gives golf and life their closely identical natures. Life allows us our ups and downs. It grants us unrest and it gives us peace. It shows us uncertainty and also certainty. The amazing thing is that golf allows us all the same kinds of experiences in our lives, no matter what our physical station might be. What we do with those experiences from there depends on each of us as individuals.

I do love this game for many reasons, but especially because it took me, on a hot September week, to Las Vegas and my life was changed forever. It is not hard to understand how the tournament victory, there in Las Vegas, got lost in the back canyons of my mind and my heart. Still I will be forever grateful to golf, because it took me there to the desert for that particular tournament. I am also happy I played well enough to make the sports section of the newspaper. I am also glad someone, either by accident or otherwise, had laid down a newspaper in the booth in which Sarah was about to sit for breakfast with her friends. Above all I am glad that golf gets the credit for changing yet another life in a positive way. I know it changed mine that day in the warm desert sun. I am not sure how many of those situations relative to that time in the desert were accidental or providence. I really do not care, but I do know that this game of golf and the game of life are truly amazing.

Thoughts often cascade through my mind
At speeds I am unable to grasp.
So is life sometimes for some.
I hope to stretch the years out and find peace
*   in them*
In lieu of deep lines in my face and on my heart.

— CHAPTER THIRTEEN —

New Equipment and Us

How many people do we know who go out and buy a new set of golf clubs thinking that their game will improve with the purchase of every new addition to their golf club arsenal? How many new metal woods and graphite irons do the golf club companies sell each year because we, the golfers of the world, believe that with each new purchase our games will improve and therefore we will be taken to a new level of golf skill? All you have to do is look at the stock market and follow the rising stars in the golf merchandising business to understand that many people believe they can get better and better with the help of all of this new equipment. I know for sure that this mind-set helps to keep the golf merchandise manufacturers in business, just as gamblers help to build and rebuild all of those grand casinos in all of the gambling areas in our country and beyond.

I have friends whose garages are filled with all makes and models of golf clubs. Most of them have caused little change, if any, in their owner's golf games. With each new modification and innovation that makes an appearance on the golf club market, those clubs are added to the endless list of equipment that only serves to clutter garages throughout golfdom. I have one friend who bought two sets of a certain type of woods, because he knew they would help his game, and he needed two sets in case one of the clubs in one of the sets got broken and/or lost. If that happened he would have a replacement at the ready for the lost or broken club. Each set cost about 2,000 dollars. Both sets are against the wall in a storage room or garage, of course not being used.

I might also add here that many times the equipment is used little because there is no instant reward or gratification immediately following the purchase of the golf clubs. Against the wall they stand like retired soldiers. When we buy equipment like that it says one of two things about us. First, the equipment is not the problem, and second, if the equipment is not the problem then something else has to be. You have three guesses. After we rule out the equipment, what is left? This game drives us to want to be perfect. It drives us to a deep sense and need for perfection. Some people are gullible enough to believe that new equipment can cause perfection to happen. We must always remember we will never be able to buy a perfect golf game, no matter what all of the advertisements on television, in those infomercials, and in the golf magazines intend to lead us to believe. Without work, dedication to the game, and certain skill levels to begin with, perfection is only a wish. There are occasions when we see a professional golfer whom we respect, talking about a certain golf club and we know that is the golf club for us. It will help us immediately, because our hero has said it would. The question I would like to ask here is: Does this big time golf professional carry that particular golf club in his golf bag? Does he actually play with that golf club?

Please do not misunderstand what I am saying here. All of this new equipment can help, but it is certainly not a cure-all for most of the problems that persist in our golf games. The old hardcore road of practice and doing so correctly, can go a long way toward that plateau out there called perfection. That means with old or new equipment. Never forget that in the area of practice one has to practice the right things in the right way and even in the right frame of mind. There is that stark reality that leads us to believe that some people—and most, I believe—can never attain perfection merely because they are not skilled enough physically or they are not dedicated enough mentally and emotionally to perfect their games.

Another major part of the ladder to perfection is patience. Some people lack enough patience to work through the down times this game puts out there in front of us. This game is difficult and anger makes it even harder, as does the expectation some have to always hit a perfect shot. There is a great deal of difference between a good shot and a perfect shot. Just look at the PGA Tour players for instance. One of them may go out there and win a major championship like the Masters, U.S. Open, or the PGA and then they most often go for months on end or even years without even being able to make a 36-hole cut. There are many reasons for this happening, but I am sure that in there somewhere is the patience factor. Down times happen to all golfers. The lucky ones are able to work through those times without going out and buying all new clubs, to cure the problems inherent in all of us who play this great game, just because that is the nature of the game of golf.

Working through those down times takes a great level of desire, dedication, and determination. We should never feel bad about not being perfect at golf or for not having the skills to be so. Those are the qualifications it takes for us to be in the majority of golfers in the entire world. You should, on the other hand, feel bad if you are not using the talents you have been given to play better and to allow yourself to have a good time playing a great sport.

It all comes down to what is inside each of us. Each of us needs to know what it is we want from this game and the degree of the desire and the level of dedication we have to achieve those goals, whatever they might be. It has been said, "Searching for anything is easy," and sometimes we feel that just any ray of sunlight in our golf game would be a plus for us. This is basically true, still our human nature does not allow most of us to be complacent. Therein lies the quest for more and more and that too is human nature calling out our names. Here enters the golf club companies who understand all too well this part of the golfer's mind and heart. We must always understand and realize this is a game capable of changing even the coldest of hearts and killing the strongest of spirits. Yet it is the greatest of games that one can choose to play on good days and bad days.

If you think that new equipment is the answer to your golf situation you could be both right and wrong. The golf club manufacturers do not want to hear this kind of talk from anyone. They keep developing new merchandise to sell to people who really believe there is a shortcut to perfection in the game of golf. They want all of us to believe there is a way to keep from slicing and hooking, by using their equipment. One company has produced a golf club that will guarantee you their driver will eliminate any chance of slicing the ball off of the tee. They know they can sell their technology because they already have. They realize P. T. Barnum was right. But in reality, there are few shortcuts, if any, to golf perfection.

Building a good golf game through work and dedication gives the golfer who is able to do this the true road to the joy and peace this game is capable of producing in most everyone's golf life. Before you go out and spend a great deal of money on all of these new gimmicks you might hear about, to bring you closer and closer to perfection, let me give you the telephone number of a few friends who already have tried those shortcuts to perfection. Their garages are filled with thousands of dollars worth of golf equipment, standing there, gathering dust. Some of them have only been used once.

They will be able to give you a better price on the equipment and the technology that helped them not get off of the spot where their golf game was last seen. Stop and think for a moment about the touring golf professionals. If there were some secret shortcuts to perfection—or just better golf games—surely they would take those shortcuts, instead of standing in the hot sun for six to eight hours at a time, hitting practice shots and making regular visits to their golf gurus, whoever and wherever they might be. Most all of them do have someone who will take them back into "the Garden."

On the contrary side of this issue, there are people who have been playing with the same golf clubs for many years and they still love them. Yet many of these people might well have benefited from new clubs somewhere along the way. Many of these people refuse to believe they could play better with new equipment or they might possibly believe that the new equipment is too costly. Though these points of view seem so far apart yet they are in reality close together, just at opposite ends of the spectrum. I, myself have used the same set of clubs for many years in the past. Yet through the years I have tested new clubs and therefore have used several sets of different makes and models of golf clubs during those years. Each time that I got new clubs, I did feel that they improved my game, but this change in clubs only happened every five years or so. In one case or two the time was even longer between changes in clubs. However, I did feel that my overall game improved with each new equipment change.

Before I purchased my last set of irons, I did an in-depth amount of research relative to the irons on the market at that particular time. I looked at most of the major lines of irons with graphite shafts. Then with a little more research I selected five sets of irons with graphite shafts that felt good to me. From there I did further testing and chose what I thought were the best golf clubs for me and not for the man in the commercial. For me they were and still are the correct irons and they did improve my golf game, in all aspects. After all, that is the supreme test, is it not? Even though they improved my game, I did feel as if the former set of irons had allowed me to play fairly well for the years in which I used them. Choosing golf clubs is one thing, but choosing the right golf clubs is indeed another thing altogether. A certain amount of research can only help us before making a purchase of golf equipment. Any decisions we make in our life, be it golf or otherwise, should be made from a logical point of view and not just an emotional perspective.

When I see someone who buys new golf clubs over and over again or when I hear someone saying without hesitation that they feel that new clubs will certainly help their game, I automatically think of names like Hogan, Hagen, Sarazen, Casper, Sneed, Thompson, Barber, McCloud, Baer, Nelson, and the list goes on and on. They did not have all of the high tech equipment at their disposal that we have in today's golf merchandise market. Nelson won eleven tournaments in a row with the same old golf clubs. Each of these champions felt good about their own golf clubs. You might say, "They had little choice." You would probably be right, but the real difference is what was inside of the person holding those clubs. These men practiced and practiced and when they needed it they got help with their game.

If you would or could talk to any of them today, they would tell you that as great as they were, they needed help many times in their golf careers. I once met Byron Nelson and as I shook his hand, the thing I found most intriguing was not the greatness of all of his golf records, even though one has to be impressed by them, but rather the firmness of his handshake and the gleam in his eye. This was many years past his prime, still the love for this game was much in evidence in him. Those golf heroes of yesteryear also had a desire, a raging fire in their bellies to always play golf as well as possible, but above all to play.

Some of these men were strict about their diets. Those aforementioned golfers, many of them were dedicated about exercise and about sleep. Some of the others, as we well know from stories and history, were not so dedicated and disciplined about those things. Yet they all had that special fire inside of them that seemed to push them toward perfection. Perfection will never happen without that desire for perfection.

Perfection may or may not happen in our lives, but it will certainly never happen without that special fire in our bellies. We may or may not all feel that special fire because it takes a special relationship with golf in order for something like that fire to occur and burn inside any of us. We need to seek out that special feeling for this game in order for that fire to occur. It goes beyond just wanting to play golf. It goes beyond just loving golf. It goes to a need to understand the unique points of this game and the questions the game of golf raises inside each of us. It takes a desire to understand the game of golf and a real love for the game. That mixture can create the often elusive level needed to find success in the game of golf. For most people that will only occur when they reach a place in their lives where they have a desire to learn more about the game of golf. When that level is attained they then might feel as if they are being pushed steps further along and/or closer than they thought they ever could be, in the quest for the perfect relationship, for them, with golf.

A friend of mine who lived in Arizona at the time of this story, had invited me to his home on several occasions. This occurred most of the time whenever he had a golf match he wanted to play against two or more friends and he needed a partner. On this one particular visit he was so excited when he met me at the airport because, according to him, he had discovered a way to make the golf ball fly further. When we reached his home I found out that his wife was away in New York City visiting some of her family. We went immediately to the kitchen where he had a brand new sleeve of Titlest golf balls sitting on the Formica table. He explained to me that he had found out that if he placed one of the new golf balls in the microwave oven for a period of thirty seconds and then removed it from the oven and dropped it on the tile floor in the kitchen, that ball would bounce higher than the others from the same sleeve of three, which had not been exposed to the microwave oven.

He demonstrated his premise to me. Low and behold the theory was a good one. When he removed the ball from the oven and he dropped the oven-toasted ball alongside the nonoven-toasted ball, from the same height, the ball from the oven bounced about 6 inches higher than the other ball did. He then decided that if the ball bounced that high with a 30-second blast from the microwave oven, then it should bounce even higher when it was exposed to the oven for a full minute.

Mr. Edison continued his quest for the perfect golf ball. He was searching for a shortcut to more distance. About 45 seconds or so into the experiment the ball exploded leaving the microwave oven in total shambles and the two us on the kitchen floor scrambling for cover. Perfection in this case of searching for more distance was thirty seconds and no more. The search for that little bit more distance called for a trip to the local appliance store to replace the microwave oven, before his wife returned from her trip to New York City.

All of the new equipment in the world will not automatically produce perfection in the golf games of any person who attempts to play this game, using that new equipment. On the other hand, if it allows us a momentary time of joy, day in and day out, that is what it is supposed to do. We should play this game because it brings us joy.

All of this shiny, wonderful equipment cannot bring perfection into our golf games unless we have a feeling of peace inside ourselves relevant to our inner self. That means peace in far more ways than just golf. I have played golf with a great number of people who act the same way, relative to golf, before and after new golf equipment has been purchased. Perfection is difficult at best and when our minds control us and our golf games it will always be the same. It is easy to love golf and love life when things are good in both of those areas of our daily goings and comings. Still when things get a bit disheveled in those areas it is often difficult to try to do what is needed to recoup those feelings and positive attitudes that had made both of them good in the past. That takes practice, not new equipment or a new heart, though they both can help in certain given situations.

It is not easy to work through our problems and that is where individual responsibility comes into play. Whatever or whoever we love, we must experience responsibility toward that area of our life in order for it to grow and mature toward perfection. That is how true emotional and spiritual culminations occur. The equipment needed for those jobs is found way down deep inside all of us, maybe. If the fire burns, for those treks toward perfection, you may or may not be strong enough to understand what that fire means or even feel it burning, for that matter. You see that is the equipment that is needed first and foremost. The price for that equipment is measured, not in dollars, but in perspiration, desire, and love. All of the new equipment in the world will not help us produce perfection without a self-imposed relationship with our inner self, as well as a special relationship with the game of golf. It takes more than buying equipment and just trying to play the game. It can be a special relationship.

> No matter whether we use a piece of steel,
> Our hands, or our minds,
> It will be better for us in the long run
> If we seek to use all of our own physical and
>   mental equipment
> To make this relationship as special as it can be.

— CHAPTER FOURTEEN —

Lessons

It would be wise to spend a bit of time here talking about golf lessons and their advantage—or not—to us who try to play this great game and better ourselves at it. I must first of all say there are people who never take lessons. They have a hundred different reasons for not doing so and when you see them trying to play the game of golf, the fact that they have never taken a golf lesson in their entire life is evident, most of the time. The good thing lessons can do for any golfer is establish, in one lesson or in a series of lessons, the proper way to attempt to play this wonderful game. The lesson or lessons can also attempt to hone specific areas of one's golf game, such as putting, chipping, iron play, or hitting the fairway metals and the driver. Lessons can teach the student the proper way to practice and a knowledgeable way to pick out the areas of one's game that need the most work. Lessons can also develop the strong sides of our game. As a matter of fact that is how the strong sides of our games are developed, through advice, from someone with an appropriate knowledge about the golf game. This has to be followed up by practice, practice, and then more practice. What is needed is practice, perseverance, and then even more practice.

The negative aspect of a golf lesson is that some people who attempt to teach golf do not understand the basic fundamentals of the golf swing and its relationship to the human anatomy. They might be wonderful players, with great skills relative to

113

the game of golf, but incapable and inadequate teachers of the golf game. Many of these people try to teach someone to play golf according to their own successes, without taking into consideration the skills and physical makeup of their individual pupils.

They try to teach every student the same way and the same things, at the same pace. That is what I call "book teaching" and that is a nonemotional approach to this emotional game. The reason this approach is so bad, so unsuccessful as well as unreliable, is that everyone is different with so many different physical characteristics, as well as emotional characteristics and reasons for trying and wanting to learn to play this game. Quite simply put, everyone is different in more ways than just one. I believe that any good teacher will approach every student as an individual. The good teacher will take into consideration all of his or her student's physical and mental makeups, which are apparent. He or she will observe the way that the student moves and flows in an attempt to create a solid golf swing. If this sounds complex, it is because the golf swing can be complex.

We had a golf professional at our golf club, at one point, who was quite well-known in the golf business and had a wonderful manner about him, as far as his personality was concerned. I would often be on the practice range near where he was giving a lesson and in earshot of the instruction area. His method of teaching always seemed the same to me. He taught golf the way he knew how to play the game. That method was good for him, but suppose his student was less athletic than he was, or heavier or taller or shorter. I am sure each of his students had different strengths and weaknesses. Each of these things are important to address when we try to learn this game and important to take into consideration when we are being instructed in how to play this game of golf.

There were times when I would be practicing there on the driving range and people would come by and ask me to have a look at their golf swings. Of course my advice is always free. I feel happy and honored, most of the time, to have someone ask me for help and I do try to help them in any way possible, if I feel I can. More times than not I can spot a swing flaw or suggest something they might try to help remedy their golf swing errors. Making some small suggestion cannot only help them play better, but those ideas might also allow them to have more fun when they do get around to playing their next round of golf.

I mention this here because one day, the aforementioned pro walked by me on the practice range after he had seen me trying to help someone with their golf swing. He was truly offended because in his mind I was taking golf lessons away from him when I helped one of the fellow members with their golf game or techniques. Because he brought the subject up I told him about my theory and what I thought about the idea of teaching everyone the same way and with the same agenda. I explained to him that everyone, at least in my mind, should be taught according to their own abilities. I wondered, at that moment, if he was sorry he had brought the whole subject up in the first place.

Strangely enough I think he understood what I was talking about. Still I continued by saying, "I make it easy for them to understand and I try to fix only the broken parts. All I get out of this is the joy that I feel from watching them feel better about their own games and about themselves. If they smile, I am happy. After all they are not training for the tour. They only want to have fun." This I think he also understood, at least I believed he did. A few days later I overheard him giving another lesson and this time it was quite different. The lesson was not generic, it was personal. He saw me and he smiled because I was smiling in his direction and then he winked at me. Man, I love this game and what it can be for all of us. That little encounter between the golf pro and me helped his students and it may have even helped him in his teaching. I know that it helped me to express my views on the matter of lessons.

What is even worse than an incapable golf instructor who is a golf professional, is a person who does not even play golf well, trying to help someone else to learn the important points of the game of golf. I have to say that the intent of such a person is to be commended, but the damage from these good intentions can be far-ranging. A person who is a 15-handicap golfer does not have the tools needed to help someone else, unless that handicap of fifteen has been brought about by injury, sickness, or age. Most 15-handicap golfers cannot remedy bad golf swings. Think about it, if they could fix golf swings then they would certainly fix their own and they themselves would not be 15 handicappers. I was playing golf with two friends one day this past summer. One was a 9 handicapper and the other was a 14. The 9 handicapper said to the 14 handicapper, "I can fix your swing," after watching his friend go through about 3 holes of pure unadulterated torment and frustration. The 14 handicapper spoke up and quickly said, "I have only one teacher and he knows my swing, so please do not try to help me. I will go to see him this week, but thanks anyway." I liked hearing this because the 14 has confidence in his teacher, whoever he is. That is what it takes to learn from someone else, confidence they can help you with your own individual golf game. Added erroneous information is only a confusing element.

One of the good things to glean from the above story is that his teacher had evidently taken the time to not only work with his student's golf swing, but he also had worked specifically with the 14's physical and mental strengths, on an oh-so-needed personal level. He had made the 14 believe in all three of those areas and therefore the golfer could use those positive aspects to his advantage, even though on occasions they do break down and need to be refixed. We must remember that all golf swings break down at some point and need to be retuned, no matter how well one plays this game. Tiger Woods is a good example. When he realizes he is not playing at his best, he does not hesitate to call on his teacher for help and he gets it. Unless you are better than Tiger Woods, golf lessons can likely help you.

Lessons are good, at least good lessons are good. Each person must decide where to find good lessons, but always make sure they are good lessons from a positive teacher. One needs to ask around about who the good teachers are and where they are. Wherever you go for lessons, make sure your needs are being met and that as you learn more you are getting better and better, and above all that you are having fun as your progress continues. Make sure your teacher is using your personal physical capabilities in his teaching and always keep in mind that you and you alone are paying for the golf lessons you are taking, and therefore you should get the most for your money. Do not pay for golf lessons to be painful and void of improvements and joy. Good lessons are indeed helpful.

As I have eluded to before, even the greatest players have their own teachers, who by the way, many of them have had since they were young. Some of the professionals do change teachers if they feel they are not getting proper help in the advice they are receiving from their teachers and coaches. Most of the teachers who have been with certain pros for a long time know how to work with their students, even though they might have three or more students out there on the professional golf tour, at the same time. They can work with them on an individual basis, because they know the players personally and therefore they are able to work with the players' own skills and personalities. The key word here is individual, because everyone is different. Does that sound familiar? The great teachers have students who come from all over the globe to seek them out. The reason for this is that they, the teachers, are able to teach their students as individuals and not as part of the masses. They make it personal. The teachers are also good at what they do because they know what they are doing. This is like seeking a specialist in the medical or surgical field. The students, our golf heroes, have to believe that their teachers know what they are doing. They have confidence in them. In 1962 Jack Nicklaus won his first official PGA paycheck. He finished tied for 50th place in the L.A. Open. His paycheck was a whopping $33.33. I would be willing to wager anyone that after that he sought help for his swing and for his mind. It worked, because golf history tells us that it did.

The story is told that Davis Love the Second took his young son, Davis Love the Third, to see a famous golf teacher in Texas. The teacher asked the father to take his young son to the practice putting area. The father, Davis Love the Second, quite a well-known teacher himself, informed the older teacher that he wanted him to look at his son's golf swing and not his putting stroke. The teacher walked to the putting green. The father quietly, with his young son in tow, followed the older man to the putting green. Then he gave his young son his putter and a number of golf balls. The teacher asked the younger Davis Love to stroke about ten balls at the hole, which was about 15 feet away. He did so and each ball rolled about 5 to 6 feet past the hole. The father proudly proclaimed, "You see, sir, I have taught my son that a ball that does not get to the hole will not go into the hole." The older teacher smiled and said in reply, "Yes, but a ball that rolls by the hole 6 feet will not go in either." This was a teacher who knew his craft.

As far as golf instructional books are concerned one must decide for himself or herself what they can learn from a book. I like some golf books, but only because they have some pretty pictures in them and on occasions they might have a good story or two about this great game. I believe that most golf instructional books have little actual swing education for us as real people because we need to be able to physically do what we read about. Personal is always better. Some people might be able to glean a great deal from books, still my time is better spent hitting golf balls and doing so in the correct manner or spending time with someone with whom I can have verbal exchange.

There are also many golf teaching videos, probably hundreds at least. The sole purpose of these videos is to make you believe they can teach you how to play golf quickly and even do so without proper practice. They are for the most part gimmicks, because their true sole intent is to make money. How could I have forgotten that? One of those video producers even stated that with his video someone would start right off playing like you were not a beginner and that could happen with absolutely no practice. Yes by just reading the information furnished to you by the company and watching the video you will play like you are not a beginner. After that you would be on your way to playing great golf. Another chance to buy one's self a good golf game, which is bogus. You remember P.T. Barnum....

In the previous chapter we talked a great deal about golf equipment and how the proper equipment is necessary if we are going to be at our best in this game of golf. The average person knows little about golf equipment except what they read about, see on television, or have been told by someone who sells equipment. One just has to try a great number of clubs to find the right ones for them and also get some help from a person knowledgeable about golf equipment. That person might be your local golf professional or someone in the golf business, such as a golf retail store salesperson who is knowledgeable about golf equipment, not just a salesperson. You must remember that most of the people who sell golf equipment are not low handicappers. Like lessons and golf teachers, not everyone who sells golf equipment knows a great deal about golf equipment. So just as we have to be careful about contracting for golf lessons, we also have to be careful about purchasing golf equipment.

A good player can hit any club, but some clubs they can hit better than others and that is an important point to make. Some people are better with steel shafts than other shafts, while others are better with graphite or fiberglass shafts. There is a great deal of emphasis made today on the amount of vibration and durability in certain shafts, as well as the distance they can provide, the feel, and the direction they are supposed to be aiding us in achieving. A golfer of any level can form a relationship with a certain set of clubs. They can also be led to believe that he or she can hit that particular set of clubs, better than any other golf club out there on the market today. That belief is called confidence. That same emotion carries over into performing certain shots that often seem psychologically difficult, such as sand shots and thin or bad lies. Confidence is the source of strength in everyone's golf game, no matter on what level you might play. If you believe this is not true, ask you favorite tour player about what it means to have confidence in their putting stroke from a mere 5 feet.

We must remember that we cannot buy a game, unless it is Trivial Pursuit or Monopoly. We most certainly cannot buy a golf game. It takes learning and a great deal of hard work to become good at this wonderful game.

To hit the fairway off of the tee time and time again is not boring, although many people laugh and ask, "Does that ever get boring?" It is something that most people would like to be able to accomplish in their own golf swing. That comes with practice and with the proper teaching from someone who knows what they are doing and what they are talking about. The same is true with one's putting stroke and with any and all of one's golf clubs from the sand wedge to the driver. Of all the strokes with which we are faced in this game of golf, the most personal of those is the putting stroke. Each person feels different about his or her putting stroke. Still good lessons on putting are also helpful. A good teacher can truly pick up flaws in all aspects of someone's golf game. That person can be a valuable resource for someone who wants to improve their golf game.

The most understanding and wonderful golf teacher I ever knew was a woman. She was constantly sought after for lessons. She was booked up for months at a time. I remember going by the club where she taught and watching her on a number of occasions. She looked so tired and as if she would just drop at any moment, yet on she went lesson after lesson. She loved to teach other people to play golf. She was so good at teaching because of her love for the game, her knowledge of the game, and because both golf and her students were personal. One day she died there on that practice range, doing what made her and so many other people happy.

Just to drop a bit of trivia here…the first practice range ever opened was in Pinehurst, North Carolina, in 1913. It was rightly named Maniac Hill. Think about that. Professional golfers would gather there to exchange ideas on teaching, and other theories relative to golf as they perceived them. That is where the true lesson tees began.

Correct lessons are good, but the bulk of the responsibility for your golf success is in your court. Sometimes no one can help us like we can help ourselves, but there are other times when we need to reach out. Remember there are the 3 Ds and the 3 Ps. Just what those numbers and letters relate to will be revealed a bit later. They are your compass to finding out about your golf game and yourself, inside and out.

The sure test of any day in which we are blessed
to live
Is not the goals we might have achieved,
But rather a lesson or two learned before that day
is done.

— CHAPTER FIFTEEN —

The Scotland Trip and My First Odyssey

It may sound strange to some people to talk about a golf trip as an odyssey, but believe me to other golfers it can sound like a dream or a fantasy. The trip I took in 1986 to Scotland was both a dream and a fantasy. I guess I have to describe this particular golf trip as an odyssey, although it seems that every time I have a chance to play a round of this great game it is, in its own way, an odyssey. Life is the same way, if we approach it from that point of view and if we can observe and understand all of the joys therein that we can take advantage of and enjoy.

I had thought for many years about going to Scotland to play golf. After all that is where it all started, all those years ago. The United States Golf Association said it best on the back cover of one of their publications. It reads as follows: "700 years ago, a shepherd hit a rock with a stick and the darn thing hasn't stopped rolling since." If Scotland is indeed the original Mecca of the game of golf, then those of us who love this game so much should come face to face with golf in its homeland and experience the wonderful thrill of a walk from here back to the beginning of it all.

I left the airport in Glasgow in my small red rental car. Once I got myself and, of course, the car on the right side of the road, or should I say the correct side of the road—that is what got me off on the wrong track in the first place—I seemed to be all right. I finally figured out that the right side of the road was indeed the left side of the road in the United Kingdom. To say the least it was touch and go for the first few minutes out of the airport rental car dealership. After those first few moments of adventure I finally found myself on the left side of the road and driving toward Prestwick.

Upon reaching that little kingdom by the sea, I promptly found the Prestwick Golf Club and I was happy to be off of the road and walking once again, on either side of the road. I went into the golf shop there at Prestwick and asked the young man behind the counter about the possibility of playing that famous old golf course the following day. I was told by the golf professional, whose name was Frank, a red-faced young man who certainly looked like he was truly Scottish, that I could come over the following morning and play there, but only after nine o'clock. I was delighted at the way this whole situation transpired, because it seemed so smooth, as if it was meant to be. After leaving the pro shop I walked directly across the street and found the nice little bed-and-breakfast Frank had recommended and there I registered for a three-night stay.

The little inn was only about a three minute walk from seashore. Later that evening, after my dinner/supper, I walked down to the water's edge and as I stood there, on that point of land overlooking the sea, I thought about how great it was to be there in the land where all of this golf business began. I was almost consumed by the feelings of raw emotion that place conjured up inside of me. The wind was rather silent in the late afternoon light and the sun was just about finished for the day. I was excited about standing on the western shore of the country where golf was born. This was thrilling and emotionally binding for me, and I was only on the edge of it all. I had only tipped the cup.

When I finally bedded down for the evening I was so excited about playing golf the next morning at Prestwick and in Scotland that I could hardly go to sleep. I felt like it was Christmas and I was a little boy once again, waiting to see just what Santa was going to leave for me under the tree, or in this case on the tee. The only thing negative about that evening was the strange meal I experienced in a small restaurant in that wonderful little village earlier in the evening. As I tried to get the music in my stomach to quiet down a bit, I felt a smile cross my lips when I thought that no matter what the food was like, "I did not come here for the cuisine." I found out later that it was indeed a good thing that I was there for the golf and not the fare. The food was going to take some getting used to for me.

The following morning, promptly at the striking of the hour of nine, I walked into the pro shop and there was Frank again. I thought to myself that he must truly put in some long, hard hours working. Once I talked to him, I found out he did put in a great number of hours. He had already assigned me a caddie, a large man in his late twenties with a strong Scottish accent. It could not have been any better for me. (Now these years later, I have found out that the caddie who carried my bag that day is now the caddie-master right there at Prestwick Golf Club.)

As my caddie and I walked toward the 1st tee I was approached by a smallish man in his early fifties, also with a strong Scottish accent. He came over to ask me if I would mind if he joined me in my round of golf. I, of course, asked him to do so, even though there was a part of me that wanted to enjoy this virgin voyage in solitude. In this country where golf was born, there are definite, though unwritten rules, about manners and etiquette when a person is on the golf course. I remember thinking that back home there are places where one goes to play golf and he or she has to be careful not to get run over by people running to the 1st tee, to get ahead of the person or group in front of them. "But this is different," I thought as the smallish man ran off to "fetch his trolley," as he said. I also noted he told me his golf trolley was in the boot of his car. I watched as he carefully removed his metal golf cart from the trunk of his car, opened up the wheels of the cart and quickly made his way back toward the 1st tee.

After our tee shots, we both could have been a bit happier, but there was little possibility that I could have been more content. I was happy, at that point, to have this gentleman, Richard, join me. "I gather by your accent that you are Scottish," I said as we made our way toward the 1st green. He smiled and looked up at me over his small wire-framed glasses, "Aye I am Scottish and thanks for not calling me Scotch, because that is good drinking whiskey, it is." I laughed at the thought of calling someone from Scotland a Scotch, although I was sure it had been done before, maybe even by me. I was also sure that I would not do it again, if I had done it the first place.

I recorded our scores on the scorecard after we putted out on the 1st hole, a 4 and a 5. I was happy that the 1st hole I had played in Scotland was played to the par on the card. "I do not live in Scotland. I am actually here to visit me Mum," Richard said, as we walked along the 2nd fairway. "I live in the northern part of California." When I told him I was also living in the northern part of California we both had to laugh, and when we compared our addresses, well you guessed it, we lived about 1 mile apart in Marin County, just north of San Francisco. This game is so great, and it never ceases to amaze me.

Richard turned out to be a nice man with a handicap of 14 or so. The entire round was one wonderful hole after another. I could not stop thinking of all of the amazing shots and feelings that must have occurred on those hallowed grounds through the years. It seemed that each hole was more interesting than the one before.

There was one hole that had the largest sand trap I had ever seen in my entire golf life and I believe it might still hold that record. Richard even took a photograph of me standing in the middle of that massive bunker, and when I had the film developed I could hardly be seen, even wearing my purple sweater. As we walked down the 18th fairway I was not feeling my usual slight bits of depression, which sometimes occur when I am walking or playing that last hole in a round of golf. The reason for that unusual feeling was simple. It was because after that morning round of golf at Prestwick. I was heading to Turnberry and another round of golf in the afternoon. As we were approaching the 18th green, my caddie pointed out to us the old clock, which we could see on the side of the clubhouse. It was one hundred or more years old, he told us. He further informed us that in a professional tournament held there at Prestwick some years before, one of the famous touring professionals from the United States skulled a shot from the greenside bunker and hit the clock dead center. That did not help Richard who, as fate or a bad swing would have it, hit his approach shot toward the green but it landed in that same bunker. He was able to get it out and onto the green without breaking anything at all, including the old clock. After paying the caddie and having a quick lunch with Richard, where we exchanged addresses and telephone numbers, I was off to the south of Prestwick and another part of that day's incredible adventure.

Turnberry, like so many of the golf courses in Scotland is situated on a rather high and rocky edge of a beautiful coastline. It looks right down into the Irish Sea. As I walked around the golf course, it reminded me quite a bit of the northern coast of California. There is a large white hotel overlooking the golf courses at Turnberry. There are two wonderful golf courses there. I was able to play the Ailsa Course, which is the longer and more beautiful of the two courses, at least this is what I was told. It is said that parts of the 2 golf courses were closed down during World War II so the fairways could be used as runways, so airplanes could bring the wounded back there from the war. The aforementioned hotel was used during that war as a hospital for the recovery and care of wounded military men and women. The wounded were flown into the Turnberry Golf Course/landing field and they were then taken to the hospital on the hill for their care and convalescence.

My caddie's name at Turnberry was Edgar, an older man, who I found out later was a younger man in reality. He had pushed his life ahead by at least twenty years or so with the drinking of scotch, ale, beer, and I am sure whatever else was there and available to him for consumption at the time. The golf course was so beautiful that I had to keep my mind on what I was doing or lose control of my golf game altogether. As we walked along the fairways I overheard the caddies telling various stories and tales about the golf course. I wondered then, as I do now, how many of those stories were true and how many of them were folklore or legend. All in all the round of golf was spectacular. Even more so than most, because of the visual wonderment that filled that late afternoon in that special and wonderful part of the world. It seemed that all was right in God's world at that point in time, at least for me.

Later that afternoon as I was driving out of the golf course parking lot, then about 7:30, I noticed Edgar was standing alongside the road trying to hitch a ride. This, I was to find out later, was normal because many of the caddies could not and cannot afford a car. Others have no driving permits for various reasons— some of which I suspect are relative to the consumption of alcohol. As I drove up to where he was standing I motioned for him to get in the car and he did. He told me he lived in a small village between Turnberry and Prestwick.

As we drove the few miles to his village Edgar explained to me why he had not accepted the beer I had offered to buy him after the first 9 holes in which I had played. The buying of a beer for one's caddie is a normal gesture from the player to the caddie. I thought that it might have been because I was drinking only a soda. He volunteered the information to me, that whiskey had truly ruined his life. He said, "Look at me, I am 38 years old and I look 65." He was right, he did look so much older than he really was. His teeth were almost all gone, but there was a bright smile hidden behind that too old, too fast face. He still had a bit of a sparkle left in his eye as he confessed to me that his wife of seventeen years had gotten him to start going back to church. With her help and the help of many people in his village and beyond, he had stopped drinking six years before. I heard somewhere that it takes a complete village to raise a child. I guess it took a complete village to save old young Edgar.

With Edgar's directions we arrived at the front of his house. It was a modest place by Scottish standards, I was sure. He invited me to go in with him and meet his family. I really wanted to go on to my bed-and-breakfast, but I also felt honored to have been given such an invitation, so I accepted. It was wonderful to meet his wife and his mother and share a nice bit of time with them. It was rewarding to get to know the other side of his family, the side which had undoubtedly saved Edgar's life.

As we sat around that evening and shared a nice yet simple meal together, I was emotionally touched because at the time right before eating the evening meal the family held hands and offered a prayer for all of their many blessings. I could not help but think about how much I really had to be thankful for in comparison. A rich blessing for me was going into their home and sharing that time with those wonderful people. Golf had allowed that to happen. I was open for it to happen.

Later that evening when I finally got around to lying down for a night of rest, I was still so involved in what that day had brought my way, it was hard again for me to go to sleep. Still this sleepless time was different than mere anticipation. I thought about just how important every part of the journey through life is. How important it was that I was able to go into Edgar's home and meet his family. I was probably the first person Edgar had caddied for who took the time to really get to know the man and his family and just maybe I was the first person for whom he had caddied, who was invited into his home for a meal. It was indeed a home and not just a house. What a perfect part of that first day of golf for me, in the land where it all started. This game is something. It gives me (us) so much. We just have to be ready to accept the gifts when they come our way.

The following morning found me driving the short distance between Prestwick and Troon. Like Turnberry, there are also 2 golf courses there at Troon. I played the unfamous Portland Course in the morning and it was all right, but nothing to get really excited about, other than where I was and what I was doing and that was truly enough to get excited about. About one o'clock in the afternoon I met up with some Americans from a golf school in San Diego, whom I had met on the flight into Glasgow from the United States. We had prearranged to play the Olde Troon Course in the afternoon and it was as advertised. The course was sort of a blend of Turnberry and Prestwick. I thought, as I was walking down the 9th fairway, that a man could truly learn to love this part of the world (when the weather was this pleasant) and this place in his mind and heart.

When our foursome reached the famous postage stamp par 3 hole, it looked demanding. The thrill for our group was that each of us hit that small green in regulation. I was to find out later that when all four players hit that special little green in regulation, it is quite a feat, all by itself. One of the caddies in the group mentioned that he had never caddied for a foursome when all four of the players hit that small green in regulation. Maybe that was true or maybe he was working for a tip, but it made each of us feel really good. Walking down the last fairway and looking out toward the sea to my left, I was feeling content and again blessed and in total communion with God's creations and man's creations too.

The funniest parts of the whole day occurred after we had nearly finished the round and either through skill, sleep or lack of both I had hit my approach shot directly into the bunker in front and right of the 18th green. As I approached the bunker, my caddie informed me that in the last British Open, which was held there at Troon, one of the golf professionals playing in the tournament had been in that same bunker and he had hit a screaming shot (skulled of course) from the bunker into the large glass window overlooking the final green. As I listened to him I wondered if the caddies at some of the more famous golf courses, might tell these stories to everyone, to make their games and days more interesting. Still I considered such a story a challenge, be it true or false. My shot was not perfect from the bunker, but I did not have to use my Visa card to replace a rather large window either.

A bit later in the clubhouse, after our golf clubs were put away and we were all relaxing and talking, I overheard the manager of the golf club speaking with an American couple. The couple seemed upset because the woman could not play golf on the Olde Troon Course. The club manager said in a strong Scottish accent: "It is in our bylaws, no dogs, no cameras, and no women. Sorry, sir." I could only imagine how that would have gone over in many places in the United States. Still rules are rules.

Later that afternoon, after a nice shower and a warm meal—this one was a good one for my stomach and for my palate—I took a stroll from the small inn down to the waterfront once again, to sort of say goodbye to that perfect little spot that I'd found in the world. I looked out at the sea, for what seemed a long time, but still too short, and I thought how great that part of the world seemed to be for me. I vowed to myself that I would return to that spot someday and look once again out to sea, and then turn and look back toward the land of golf's birth. It seemed the place to be and not necessarily the place to be alone. I kept that promise.

The next morning I arose early and before the sun had heated the day, I was on the road, biding farewell to the western shore of Scotland, at least for a while. I had prearranged, through a friend of mine in Aberdeen, to play the Muirfield Golf Club. The drive was nice and surprisingly fast. I stopped a few miles from Muirfield and telephoned the golf club to make sure that my reservations were intact and of course they were. The manager of the club, "the Major" was how they addressed him, informed me they were anticipating my arrival. He said, "Please do not eat lunch before arriving here, because we have a great lunch buffet."

Since I was only a short distance from the golf course at Muirfield when I had telephoned there and I had plenty of time on my hands, I decided to look around for something to do and I found it. It was called the Gullane Golf Course. The course was nice, but I was so looking forward to playing at my next stop, I really did not give Gullane Number 1 a chance to excite me. Yet it was a wonderful way to spend the late morning hours there in East Lothian. That stop was not without its moments of joy; after all I was playing golf.

The lunch at Muirfield was indeed as advertised. There was a bit of every kind of food from that region and far beyond. After lunch, the Major escorted me personally to the caddie-master and informed me on the way there that they had only one golf cart, which was available for me to use. I thanked him for his consideration of my leg, but I explained to him that all I really needed was a caddie. That seemed to please him. He was a gracious host with a happy heart and a true scottish complexion, much akin to Frank back at Prestwick.

My caddie had caddied for Paul Azinger when the British Open had last been played there at Muirfield. I only learned this because the caddie himself told me. He also told me he was a 1-handicap golfer. I had no reason to disbelieve him, besides it did not matter to me either way. Both stories could have been truth or fable. It made no difference whatsoever to me. The golf course was nice, but the wind was a bit Scottish. I kept thinking to myself all the way around the golf course that it could not get any better than what I was experiencing. Many times when I say that, I find out I am often wrong in that assumption. When the Major first offered me the golf cart his only instructions were as follows: "If you need the buggy it is here, but please do not drive it in the rough." As I left Muirfield that afternoon I had to laugh at the way we in America approach things and how that differs so many times from the Scottish sense of direction. I know neither side is wrong, but the variety sure is nice. We, in America, would prefer someone drive a golf cart in the rough rather than in the fairway. The Scottish sense of order would choose to preserve the rough because it gives their golf courses much of their character. I like it both ways. It is golf, you know.

Later that afternoon, after a wonderful day of golf, I drove the short distance to St. Andrews. With the help of the tourist bureau I found a small bed-and-breakfast and there I stayed for three nights. The following morning, early, with my golf bag on my shoulder, I went in search of the "Old Course," which was only two short blocks from where I was staying. As I walked along the streets of the old town of St. Andrews they were wet from rain, which must have fallen in the night; but in those early morning hours there were no clouds to be seen anywhere. Once I was there at the golf course, on that sacred ground, I inquired about the possibility of playing golf that morning. The starter encouraged me to come back in the afternoon, if that would be possible, and try to play with one of the members. I felt his suggestion was a good one, so off I went in search of another place to play. I found it too, Lundin Links. A beautiful little spot right on the water with 9 holes going out and 9 coming in. A true links course indeed.

I finished the morning round in time to reach St. Andrews by my appointed hour. When I approached the starter, for the second time that day, he suggested that I go over and ask two rather dapper looking gentlemen on the putting green if I might join them in their afternoon round. "Go and ask the two mem-

bers there if ye might join them in their round," he said in a soft
Scottish voice, almost whispering. I followed his instructions once
again and went over and introduced myself to the two gentlemen. They were kind and offered me the chance to join them in
their afternoon of golf. One of these men was a barrister and the
other was a clergyman. That's right, a lawyer and a preacher.
That is quite a combination, but I must admit that I have played
golf with a lawyer before, on occasions.

After an enjoyable round of golf they invited me into the
old club house to join them for a drink. It felt really special and
above all, right to walk on that hallowed ground. It was wonderful to sit in that place where literally the kings of golf have
convened, since the beginning of golf itself, at least as the history of golf has been recorded for us to know about. It is hard to
be there and not put all of this in some kind of realistic perspective. I realized, sitting there, that looking at all of the trophies
and plaques that adorn the cases, walls, and shelves in that old
clubhouse, makes it near impossible not to drift back to the times
when Bobby Jones and those before him and after him, walked
through that place with the mantel of victory draped upon their
shoulders. That is truly a sacred place, as it relates to this great
game.

Before the evening was over and I had finished at least two
ginger ales, I had another invitation to play again the following
afternoon with this likeable duo and of course I accepted. The
following morning I was up early and off to the golf course again.
I wanted to play the new course in the morning, if that was
possible. It was and I did, and then I had another wonderful
afternoon with the minister and the barrister. I ask for some
guidance from my two playing partners as to where I should go
from there to play the following day. They were helpful and so
the next morning I was off to Carnoustie and the windy shores
of the easterly sea. I had been informed by the minister that his
parish was on the road to Carnoustie and as I drove along in the
early morning light I kept a close eye on the landmarks given to
me by the minister.

Finally I came to the little church and I felt a real need to
stop and spend a moment there inside of that pretty little build-

ing. I had so many things to be thankful for, I could not pass up the chance to say thank you one more time. The churches there in that part of the world are not always locked, another difference from the United States. I was glad that I spent those few minutes there in the solitude and coolness of that old place of worship. Yes it was surely that for me, in those early morning hours.

When I arrived at the golf course in Carnoustie I noticed there was a rather large bus unloading many tourists. They all had expensive golf bags and of course cameras hanging around each of their necks, so I rushed into the golf shop and the young man behind the counter instructed me to grab a caddie and hit the links "and pay me later," he said. That is what I did and just ahead of the invasion. The wind was blowing in my face on the outbound 9 holes. There were short par 4 holes where I could not even reach the green with 2 woods. Yet on the inbound 9 I was able to reach both par 5s in two shots. The wind certainly makes a difference in the way those seaside golf courses play. Again I was totally absorbed by the naturalness of those 18 holes. After purchasing a sweater and finally paying my green fee, I bid farewell to the eastern coast of Scotland, at least for a while.

That evening I drove to the Highlands and played the King and Queen's Course the next day. Such a contrast from the courses I had already played along both the east and west coasts of Scotland. The contrast made the two areas, the coasts and the highlands, seem like two different worlds. From there I drove to Inverness. I made my only eagle of the entire trip through Scotland there and it was there that I shot my only subpar round of the trip. On the 12th hole I took my umbrella out of its sheath for the first time since I had been in Scotland. I smiled as the rain fell on the top of my umbrella merely because I had played many holes of golf in Scotland, to that point, without any rain. I was not about to complain. As I pulled my golf "trolley" along the fairway, through the rain, I was smiling all the while. The rain lasted for two holes and then it was gone. Before that little rain shower came I was beginning to think that I had brought my rain suit and umbrella all that way from California for nothing. I was still not complaining, as I recognized the immense mental peace granted to me by the entire trip, at least through those first days there in the kingdom of golf.

From there I traveled up the western finger of coastline to Dornoch. In Dornoch I played the Royal Dornoch Golf Club. Again the golf course was situated on such a beautiful strip of land adjacent to the water. I had really begun to understand both the beautiful and near divine reasons but also the demonic reasons for the building of golf links. They all are special and spectacular in their own way. It had been another wonderful day and the village was so pretty and unique that I decided to spend the night there in the village of Dornoch. I found a nice room in an old converted castle. They served dinner at one particular hour and everyone had to wear a coat. It was quite nice and for a change elegant. After dinner I walked around the little town. I stopped for a while and watched a number of people participating in lawn bowling. I must have sat there on that old stone wall for an hour or more and watched all of that part of the world rush slowly by. The wall on which I was sitting was probably older than the United States. It was there I realized that in all of the time I had spent going from place to place in Scotland, because of the length of the days, in that part of the world at that time of the year, I had yet to see the darkness. In some cases that is good, but the night is also special. The days were so long that I always went to bed before dark, which occurs around ten thirty or so, and then I arose after dawn. For the golfer and golf, this is perfect and to that point that was truly how everything had been.

The next day I arose early as usual. I drove down off of the finger of land where Dornoch is located and then north to the little town of Narin. It was late in the afternoon when I arrived there so I found a hotel and a snack and soon went to bed. About five in the morning I awoke, merely because I had slept enough, and I found my way to the Narin Golf Club. When I arrived at the golf club, of course there was no one around, so I just put my golf clubs on a trolly and off I went. "What a place to spend Sunday Morning," I thought as I walked along, watching the early birds fly and dart here and there in search of an early meal or two. When I finished my round and I had paid my green fees, it was still only ten o'clock in the morning. (How many places in America can we play and then pay? I am sure that they are few and far between.) As I drove away from the golf course I looked at the beautiful marshes that surrounded the golf course and thought that I should find a place to worship, even more so than I already had. I did just that. "For art may err, but nature cannot miss." John Dryden was still correct.

Since it was Sunday I easily found a small church in Narin and filled yet another need. After the service was over I decided to find something to eat, which I did, and then I also found a lovely and busy park. It was such a beautiful afternoon and I knew there was nowhere else to play golf until the following day. I took my greasy fish and chips and pulled a large towel from the boot of the car (you see how quickly I learn) and I proceeded to dine in that pretty little park. There was a cricket match being played in one end of the park and in the distance I could hear a German band playing. I sat between the two events, ate my fish and chips, and felt blessed in a special way. When the eating was over, I lay back on the big towel—listening to all of the sounds around me, watching the large white clouds dancing around far above the earth at the direction of the wind—and I enjoyed a wonderful nap.

The following day I drove around the north coast of Scotland and arrived in Aberdeen ahead of schedule, and of course I looked for and found a golf course. There I played a short little course by the name of Ballater. It was short, but sweet. After that round I telephoned some friends living there in Aberdeen, who were expecting me to stay in their home. With their instructions I found their house. The reason for going to Aberdeen in the first place was to join in the festivities of a wedding, to be held later in the week.

While I was there I played the Royal Aberdeen Golf Club twice and found it to be as beautiful as any golf course I had played during my odyssey there in Scotland. I also played a unique golf course by the name of Cruden Bay. It was built on this very high precipice overlooking the sea. From one of the greens it looked to be 1,000 feet above the sea. As I drove in the direction of the golf course that day I knew it was going to be cold, because it was overcast and looking like rain. At one place on the golf course it was truly a beautiful spot on God's earth, but the wind was screaming like banshees from a cold and windy hell. I realized that there were no banshees in hell, no golf courses there either and, from what I had heard, it is less than cold there also. I smiled to myself because it was good to believe in positive things relative to spiritual matters and not always negative things.

On one par 3 hole, which was 159 yards, with the wind in my face, I hit a fairly good tee shot. The ball rolled up onto the apron of the green. I guess it was a fairly good shot, but I had hit it with a 4 wood. Yes the wind was strong and cold. I stood there high on that windy hill and thought of all of the wonderful places where this great game had taken me in the past few days alone and I realized once again, that I, among all men, am truly blessed. Still as I stood there on that cold spot I realized why the green fees were so inexpensive and why there were few players, if any, on the golf course. I had seen no one else that entire round. Then I remembered seeing only one car in the parking lot on my arrival.

Maybe they were smarter than I was or maybe not.

That is nearly all of the odyssey, except that I played a golf course in Musselburgh, which, according to my caddie at the king's course, is truly the oldest of all of the Scottish golf courses. I guess that means the oldest golf course—period. When you think about that and you are walking there, it is awesome to realize you really and truly might be where it all started. To me it does not matter which course is the oldest, but to someone there in the land of the beginning of golf, I am sure it is a difficult test for golf history and of course, those important bragging rights. Still as I walked around that little golf course I found myself there with the shepherd, in those days long ago, standing on the grassy knoll and waiting my turn to hit the rock, which has never stopped rolling to this day. It is so easy to daydream sometimes and especially in a place that spawns enchantment..

After the wedding I left Aberdeen in the early hours of the morning and at last I saw the darkness. I was en route to Glasgow and an airplane that would take me home from this almost unbelievable journey through time and places. I had played over

340 holes of golf and I had only been rained on twice, and that for a total of 3 holes. The time was so special, that as I write these words, I still can feel both warm memories and the chill of the drive through the Highlands at two o'clock in the morning surging through my mind and heart. As the car began to climb higher into the mountains the snow began to fall. The flakes were large and they were falling straight down because there was absolutely no wind whatsoever. As I rounded a curve in the road there stood a great stag right in the middle of the road. I hit the brakes to keep from running over him and he just looked straight into the headlights of the car. His rack of antlers was massive. Then quickly he leaped across the road and after he did he stopped again and looked back in my direction, as if he had something to say, before he once again darted away into the forest. I am sure that there is nothing strange or even mystical about a deer crossing in front of a car in the middle of the Highlands at night, but I had never seen a pure white deer before. You can believe that I was really awake for the remainder of the trip down to Glasgow.

Before my flight departed for home, I telephoned my friends in Aberdeen from the airport to thank them for their kindness and to tell them about my trip to Glasgow and what I had seen. They had never seen or even heard of any white deer living in the Highlands. Well, not only did I hear about a white deer in the Highlands, I saw one with my own eyes.

The deer was a sign to me that the odyssey was indeed not over, but only beginning. He, wherever he is in the forests of the Highlands today, was right, because on and on it goes, as if it will never stop. I guess the old adage, "There are no endings, just discoveries," is true, because I see them and find them time and time again.

> *An odyssey is in many ways*
> *A voyage of the mind as well as the body.*
> *I am on an odyssey*
> *And so far it has been a voyage of both for me.*
> *The odyssey continues…*

CHAPTER SIXTEEN

The Mental and Physical Aspects of This Great Game

According to USGA records every year there are more and more people starting to play golf, not only here in the United States, but in many other parts of the world. I have been told by friends of mine who live in Germany and who have in the past year or so started trying to learn the game of golf themselves, that there are quite a number of new courses springing up all over that country. They tell me that in the Berlin area alone there are courses being built, one after the other. I also have a Swiss friend who just spent two weeks playing golf in Turkey. He told me there were four golf courses within 6 miles of the hotel where he and his wife were staying. We in this country have witnessed and are witnessing the boom of the golf business like no other place in the entire world.

In many other places around the world, other than the British Isles of course and a few other countries like Spain, the golf explosion has just begun to take place. Golf courses are being built in Indonesia and in Venezuela. In Finland alone there are 91 golf courses. One of those golf courses is in both Finland and

Sweden. You can tee off in one country and putt out in another. Just to show you how many courses are being built, as of January 2000 Jack Nicklaus has had a hand in designing over 167 courses and he has 57 more in various stages of creation. Those numbers are staggering when you take into consideration the number of golf course designers that are out there building and designing golf courses, all over the world. In 1998 over fifty million people were playing golf around the world.

Many people are finding that golf is now finally becoming affordable; it is fun and it is also a definite challenge. I believe that most of those people who find golf to be a challenge approach it as a mountain to climb, while others feel it is a good time to get some exercise and a good time to have social interaction with friends and even family. Then there are others who strive to achieve the competitive level that golf alone can offer those who would try to take it to that plateau.

Golf can indeed be a game of exercise if we work at it by walking all of the time when we play. Yet the shakers and movers in the sport of golf are working on their game by trying to get more people playing the game and playing it faster, by the use of golf carts. Their thinking, and rightly so, is that golf carts will allow more people to play each golf course and therefore generate more revenue for the powers that be. Those powers that be include, of course, cart manufacturers and cart dealers. Most every golf course makes an incredible amount of money just from golf cart rentals. Most of the new golf courses, either under construction or completed in the recent past, have been constructed in a manner that makes it difficult, if not impossible, to walk the golf course, simply because of the distance between the greens and the next teeboxes. Many times that distance is greater in total yards than was the previous hole played. To go from one green to the next teebox one many times has to travel over a road or through a development of houses, or some other such obstacle. Of course the USGA and the PGA have a hand in all of this somewhere. Still the main reason that walking is being eliminated is because of the need to make more money, and the main source of that revenue comes from getting more people playing the game of golf and riding in golf carts when they do play. It just goes back to the old basic need to generate revenue.

Yet with all of this said, golf is still a physical game. It takes a certain amount of stamina to play 18 holes of golf or more in a given day and still keep your physical strength at a manageable level. It is not at all unusual for someone to be playing fairly well, for their handicap level, to a certain point in a round of golf and all of a sudden they might have a 2 or 3 hole run where they seemed to have fallen asleep. That is exactly what has happened—of course not literally asleep. Be it the heat or just being tired, we many times do fall into a place mentally of not being able to maintain our focus on what we are doing. It happens to everyone and at all levels of golf skills. I have felt that same level of sluggishness when I was tired or I had played a great number of rounds of golf in a short span of time. I have stood over a shot and forgotten what I was doing and just hoped that my muscle memory would take over. Very seldom does that muscle memory understand what its job really is. If it does, it is merely luck.

I recently played in a Northern California PGA event and I went through a whole day of not hitting many good shots at all. Later that day, in my hotel room, as I replayed that round in my mind (something many people tend to do from time to time) I thought about how poorly I had played throughout that first day of competition. Suddenly I realized I was just plain tired, physically, emotionally, and competitively. I was awake and walking around, but I was fast asleep. Being aware that this can happen to us and to our game makes us more aware indeed of its possible entrance into our lives.

Some people might remember, many years ago watching Ken Venturi walking up the 18th fairway of the Congressional Country Club with a white towel draped around his neck. He was literally staggering as he walked, from the intense heat and from being just physically exhausted. He was struggling, as I am sure the other competitors also were, but I remember him because it was on that extremely hot day that he won the U.S. Open Golf Championship. That was a day of physical challenge for everyone who played in that event. That day golf was truly a physical sport. A person with little physical strength cannot endure that kind of trauma—very few can. After winning the 1922 U.S. Open by a single shot, Gene Sarazen said, "All men are created equal. Today I am just one stroke better than the rest." He was correct. He was a step above them all, mentally and physically on that particular day, which gave him the one stroke advantage that he needed for the victory. That is how winners win most of the time.

In 1931 the longest playoff in golf history occurred at the Inverness Golf Club. It was the U.S. Open and the two men who were tied after regulation play in the quest for the championship were George Von Elm and Billy Burke. The following day they went out to play a 36-hole playoff. After that day of play, as fate would have it, they were still tied and had to play another 36 holes the following day. After the second 36 holes of playoff action, Billy Burke finally won the 1931 U.S. Open by a single stroke. I have two questions relative to that experience for those two men. First, were they physically fit? Second, in their minds and bodies was the game of golf, at that time in their lives, a physical sport or not?

Let us, for a moment, take into consideration something more than just going out for a round of golf. Most golfers realize it takes a great deal of physical character to stand on the driving range, hour after hour, hitting ball after ball in search for that elusive perfect golf swing. That means hitting balls first with the short irons and then with the mid- and long irons and then with the fairway woods and on to the driver. It takes physical strength and character to just stand out there in the hot sun or the cold wind, practicing for hours chipping and putting to find that feel with those clubs that would allow us to have a level of confidence that is comfortable, and therefore ready for use at our next attempt at hitting some particular shot. It takes physical character to drag ourselves out of the car, after a long day's work, to practice some or all of the above-mentioned shots. It takes that same basic ingredient to set the alarm clock for six in the morning on weekends, to practice before playing that day or *instead of* playing that day. Then after the round it takes desire to go back to the range for more refinement. That takes real physical character. That takes desire.

Often we are so attuned to playing golf and riding in golf carts that we forget the parts of golf that are physical. Many of the professional tour players today have their own special physical trainers. Those trainers are not there for swing theories, but rather they are a part of the player's need for physical training and the tuning of his or her body. Most of the modern tour players understand the need to stay in somewhat good physical condition. As we watch them, it is easy to see who realizes the need and the importance of good physical awareness, and who does not spend that much time working on that aspect of their golf game or their life.

The body will tire easily if it is not in some kind of proper condition. I would like to think that most people are smart enough to know if they are in physically good shape or not. That will become obvious to us if we play or try to play golf long enough. We all know that situps and various other stretching exercises are not only good for us as golfers, but they are also good for us as human beings. If we think about some of the players from yesteryear who are either retired now or who have moved on to the Senior Tour, some of them were rather portly. The players who have come along in these more recent years seem less rotund. Of course there are exceptions to both sides of that standard. I recall stories about Gary Player in his younger years, how he exercised every day. In those days he was the exception and today he would not be. The tour players today seem more aware of their physical health, at least from their appearance it seems so. Their bodies keep them in the money so to speak.

There are many people today, who play golf in constant pain merely because this is a physical game. We use our muscles, our

tendons, our joints, ligaments and our bones. Most of the people
with whom I play golf have to use anti-inflammatories to keep
the pain in their shoulders, hands, and backs from becoming so
acute as to prohibit them from playing this great game at all.
The physical aspects of golf are certainly not the same as football or chess, but do not for one minute ever think this game of
golf is not a physical one. A young man recently broke onto the
scene of the professional golf world because he is a tour quality
player and because he has a physical disability. His disability
will probably allow him to walk for only a few more years. As he
walks now it is obvious he is in a great deal of physical pain from
his condition. Casey Martin is a wonderful golfer and a fine young
man who loves this game so much. If you think for one minute
that this game is not a physical one then you watch him, if you
ever get the chance, trying to walk from the golf cart—which he
has won the right (through the courts) to use in PGA events—
to his golf ball. What he does and what he accomplishes takes a
great deal of physical strength and character. He does not want
anything, except to be able to play this game, which we all love.
You can bet that he sets his alarm in the mornings early to get to
the practice range, just to hit balls.

If you ever for one minute think this game is not physical
and that the physical aspects of this game are not important,
then happy golfing. You will soon see the error of your ways.

The mental aspects of this game are almost too numerous to
try and mention in these few pages, but it is necessary to try.
They vary from love to hate and cover everything in between
those two emotions. They go from total emotional levels of domi-
nation to levels of being dominated. They include fear, worry,
anxiety, and just plain daydreaming. We have fun playing golf
and we get angry playing golf. We watch with tears running down
our cheeks and with laughter on our faces, as the events of golf
unfold before our own eyes and in our hearts.

Some people approach this game the same way every day
that they are fortunate enough to play the game. They practice
the same way on days set aside for only practice as they do on

the days they go out and play. Somehow, somewhere deep in their minds, some people believe that the same routine used over and over again will prevent them from becoming disconnected from the way their game was the last time they played well. If you'll recall, I mentioned in an earlier chapter some of the exercises I used while in Vietnam, just to keep me connected to the game of golf. They did just that. This is all part of the mentality that can and should be ours, relative to this game.

Everyone is somewhat different in how they mentally approach the game of golf. We believe that good luck and bad luck sometimes ride the waves of repetition. Many people mark their ball on the green with the same coin they have used since they first felt that particular coin brought them good luck. That coin is a vital cord or connection between good and bad luck, if only in their minds. Some people will not walk under a ladder, or when a black cat crosses in front of their car they have a need to go through some sort of a ritual to cleanse away that act of the cat's crossing in front of their car. By doing this they feel the act of cleansing will prevent any bad luck from coming their way. That is the same mind-set that fills the minds of people who are superstitious about using the same coins and marking their golf balls in the same fashion at each point it is needed. These people usually play the same kind of golf ball and even wear the same kind of golf glove, and the list goes on and on.

This I might add, does not just exist in the amateur ranks. It has been said that "A mind is a terrible thing to waste," and the mind can truly float or sink one's golf game. Let us look at "the Shank" as an example. Some fear a shank so much that they even have a hard time just using the word in casual conversation. They might call the shank "a lateral" or something other than what it is. That is a bad shot, a shank. I was going to play in a two-ball championship in New Jersey some years ago and I knew many of the competitors who were going to be there and participating in that event. I wrote the following little memo as sort of a joke and maybe even a scientific experiment to see just how people might be affected by small seeds of suggestion.

The Shank

According to Mr. Webster the word shank has a variation of meanings, nineteen of them to be exact. It is not surprising that the last of these definitions is the one which relates and pertains to golf and that wonderful, long lasting feeling and experience known to golfers of discernment as "The Shank." It makes me wonder that since the definition of the shank, as it relates to golf, is the last one in the Book Of Webster, if he ever played golf and hit a few of those laterals himself. He explains: "To hit (a golf ball or shot) with the extreme heel of the club so that the ball goes off in an unintended direction."

When I read this I know that there is no greater feeling than starting a much anticipated round of golf with friends, by hitting a beautiful drive of 250 yards right down the center of the fairway. That is such a joyous feeling. Then as you approach your ball for your second shot, with no more than an 8 iron in your hand, you less than deliberately with your backswing and foreswing reach the ultimate success known to golfers of distinction as the "The Shank."

Oh, one can learn to play "The Shank" by merely turning your body 90 degrees to the left of the intended target and proceed to hit the ball in the same fashion as was previously the case. Now for left handers, you have to turn the same amount of degrees, but in the opposite direction.

You see there are solutions to this wonderful experience known as "The Shank." My feeling is why bother because the feelings which result from this utopian plateau are so moving that they are ALMOST beyond words, but not thoughts.

The best way to deal with the need some people have of being absent of "The Shank" is to keep it completely out of mind. This little memo has only one service and that is to remind any who might read it, of the need they have, to forget all about "The Shank."

Have fun today and have a good round, remembering that "The Shank" can be fun. Think about it.

A Friend

As I said, writing this piece and sharing it with some acquaintances was done as a joke, but also done as a test as to the mental strength of those people, whom I knew, would be playing in the golf tournament. It is obvious the memo can be quite suggestive. On the first day of the tournament, during a pre-teeoff luncheon I handed a copy of this memo in an envelope to each of the people I knew there at the luncheon. Some of the people read the memo and laughed at the words, while others frowned. There were some of those inductees into the Shank Hall of Fame who read only the top line and threw the memo to the floor, as if it were hot or covered with some deadly modern-day virus. Later that day, the foursome in which I was playing, was standing on the 18th tee and through the small tract of trees to our left was the 11th hole. We all had a good laugh because from the direction of the 11th hole came a scream that could have literally pierced the eardrums. "I am going to kill Corbin Cherry when I see him!" We must understand first and foremost that the seeds of suggestion are strong, as a friend and as a foe, in this game merely because this is a mental and cerebral game that we have taken a liking to. Actually there is a cure for the shank and it is found in the dictionary. Think about it; after all that is what makes golf what it is.

There is also another mental phenomenon known to many golfers as the Yips. The word Yips is another one of those words that some people (golfers) do not even want to have mentioned in their presence. I watched a golf program recently on which many of the touring professionals were asked to describe or discuss the Yips. Many of them did not even want to talk about the subject. Many professionals, as well as amateurs through the years, have fallen victim to the yips. The yips occur mostly in the putting stroke. It seems that at some point in the putting stroke there occurs a sudden jerk in that stroke causing the putter face to accelerate through the putt. I have read that Chi Chi

Rodriguez, along with Johnny Miller and Tom Watson, had extremely bad cases of the yips. Johnny Miller said that at one point he got so bad that he tried putting using one eye. Then he tried using the other eye. He even tried putting with his eyes closed. He tried putting by only looking at the hole. Tom Watson supposedly had the yips for eight years. Many players have changed putters many times to find the solution, which more times than not has nothing to do with the putter or putters. Many players went to long putters, as Cory Pavin did, to try and escape the yips. Ben Hogan, it is said, quit playing competitive golf because of the yips. This is as mental as it gets. This does not just affect amateurs. It can invade anyone's game and anyone's mind.

There are people against whom we might be playing at some point who will say things to us like, "You have never missed a putt like that in your entire life," or they might say something like, "You could stay up all night trying to miss a putt like that one." These are merely mind-benders, which have been put out there to get an opponent thinking about his or her game. They are also there to dilute the process of our opponent's thought mechanisms. The mind plays games on most, if not everyone who plays this game. We must try to understand the strengths of both the bright and dark sides of this game to survive it. Those who survive the mental aspects of golf survive, period. That is true in golf and life in general.

If the mind were not such a strong part of this game of golf, then there would not be clubs in our golf bag and shots in our golf game that we are more uncomfortable with than others. We would not be so hesitant about hitting certain shots, for instance a flop shot, or hitting a ball over a rather inviting lake. Some people will not try hitting a new golf ball over a body of water, for they fear the loss of the new golf ball. They do not fear the loss of the stroke, but rather the loss of the golf ball. How many times have we—or someone we were playing with—upon reaching a water hole, gone into our golf bag for an old ball? That particular action speaks volumes about the confidence of the person with his hand in the golf bag searching for that old ball and the situation in which the lack of confidence is presenting in his life, at that moment. I cannot imagine that many good shots follow that kind of personal trial and drama. If one thinks he will not hit a good shot, only luck will allow a good shot to happen. That level of the mind, as it relates to golf, at that point is only a level of negativity. While it is true that by playing an old ball over the water, or at least trying to, some worry has been taken away, relative to the loss of the new golf ball. Still there is a dramatic shortage of confidence with the decision to hit the old ball instead of the newer one. Even though hitting an old ball is a definite indication of weakness and a severe lack of confidence, the golfer who decides to take that tack is probably better off playing the old ball, because he will be more relaxed when playing that old ball than he would have been hitting the newer one. I guess the question is,"Is it better for them to be better off now or later?" The answer is not hitting an old ball instead of a new ball. The answer is getting to a place where one can look beyond the water hazard to the fairway or green. To not even see the water is a wonderful place to be and of course, it is the best place to be. I read the following message in a golf publication and I feel that it does show what may be going on inside each of us at sometime in our golf life.

> *"There is a feeling inside of you that is aware*
>   *of fear.*
> *There is a side of you that is insecure.*
> *There is a part of your brain that thinks too much.*
> *Yet there is a part of you that is brave and even*
>   *courageous at times.*
> *You can play alone, because you are a foursome."*

All of these elements make up important parts of the golfer's mind.

I have also observed people on the practice range who will search through their golf bag for an old ball, if their last practice

shot on that day was a bad one, merely because they do not
want their last shot to be a bad one. There is a true subconscious
fear that if they hit a bad shot as their last shot on the practice
range then that will be the swing that will appear on the 1st tee
the next time they go out to play. It is all so psychological.

Superstition is a strong adversary at all levels of golf. This is
true in most sports, if not all of them. We did mention superstition
just a bit earlier, but to show you how this works on people's
minds, some people will only putt a ball when the logo on the
ball is facing a certain way. Some people cannot putt if there is
any distraction in eye view of their stroke. I can understand that
because that glimpse takes one's mind off of the business at
hand, which of course is to make a good stroke and a good putt.
The mind says to the hands, "Suppose he moves." I personally
can relate to this situation. I have asked people with whom I am
playing golf, to move from behind my putt when I am address-
ing the golf ball to putt, so I would not see them in my peripheral
vision. Therefore I do not have to concern myself, as I stand over
the putt, if they are going to move or not as I stoke the putt. The
other player may have on a yellow shirt or a red one and the
colors might cause a major distraction to one's sight. The mind
starts to roam and if there is anything the mind does not need, it
is more help in its roaming process. We are back to the mental
part of the golf game and we can see just how important it is. I
want to interject here the whole process of invoking God's help
in making a putt. By that action, as good as the intent might be,
it takes a person's mind off of the putt or the shot still left to be
hit. The mind does not need any more help in wandering. It is
capable of doing that all on its own.

Ben Crenshaw, a player of remarkable talent on the PGA
Tour, once said, "I am about 5 inches from being an outstanding
golfer. That is the distance my left ear is from my right ear." He,
at the time of that statement, was most likely having doubts
about his mental strength and not his physical skills. This is the
same man who owns the worst playoff record of anyone on the
PGA Tour. He is 0 for 8 lifetime. I am certain remembering the
fact of that record is no help for the mentality aspect of his golf

game either. Yet we all watched and cheered as he walked up that 18th fairway at Augusta National to a Masters victory. The mind is such a decisive tool in our approach to this, the greatest of games.

In 1938 Ben Hogan was playing on the PGA Tour and he was nearly broke. The night before the final round of an event in which he was playing, someone stole the tires off of his car. It is said that he sat with tears streaming from his eyes and said, "I can't go another inch. I am finished." The next day he went out and shot 69 to finish second in the tournament. He collected a check for 380 dollars, and from there he kept right on going straight into golf history.

In 1931 the PGA Championship was won by a man named Tom Creavy. In 1934 he finished 8 in the PGA Championship and after that he was never heard of again. In the 1998 British Open there was a young man from England who finished high in the competition and not yet out of his teens. After his wonderful finish there he decided to quit school and turn professional. In the next fourteen tournaments he entered, he never got past the 36-hole cut. These cases do not reflect the need for greater golf skills, but they do highlight the need for more and better mental strengths. All of the above-mentioned players were and are blessed with great physical skills. Some rose up mentally and others did not, at a certain point in their careers.

Many people often play games inside of their own heads to try and make themselves mentally tougher. We fantasize that we can play in some golf tournament and that while playing in that event, we will do well enough to springboard us into still a bigger and better tourney somewhere down the road. We try to get comfortable with our confidence level, because we know that confidence is mostly mental and above all else it is most likely a necessity. If we feel we cannot make a 3-foot putt, then the chances are pretty good that we will not make that putt with any consistency. If we feel, in our minds that we cannot hit a sand shot, then we most likely will not hit that sand shot correctly and with consistency. If this occurs, then there might be two solutions, the first of which is that we might try changing our thinking (mental) process, as it relates to those shots. That means you might need to seek help from a person with knowledge of such things, in order for that to happen. The other solution is do not and I repeat do not hit the golf ball into the sand trap.

Our minds control how we approach the game of golf, as far as practice is concerned, as far as our stroke (with all of the clubs) is concerned, as far as our choosing the proper club for a certain shot is concerned. Our minds control our patience level and our actual scoring on the golf course. Our mind actually controls the entire ball game for us. If we play well and have fun, both in the same round of golf, we have most probably had a mountain top experience. Golf or life can offer little more than this, at least to me.

In my golf life there have been a few people with whom I have talked, who have told me that on certain occasions they could truly feel a good shot coming on. They explained to me that on those occasions they actually could visualize the shot before it even happened. There is nothing dark, sinister, or occult about this level of golf, but there is something mental and special about this whole process and experience. As a matter of fact that is basically all that it is. These people are able to see the shots before they strike them because they have a certain amount of confidence that they can do what they are attempting to do. They have attained a mind plateau that allows them to believe they can do what they feel that they see. Confidence...If a person holds up two fingers most people when looking at those two fingers will only see the two fingers. Yet if we look beyond the two fingers, we can see four fingers and a great deal more than just the fingers themselves. So it is with one's golf game and our confidence in that game. We can see into a place where we can go, with the help of confidence and a sound mental approach to the game of golf. I believe that seeing a shot before it happens is the result of looking beyond the shot to before it is hit and allowing structural visualization to take place.

There are some people who play this game of golf who are of course, far more talented than those of us who labor meekly in the vineyards of mediocrity. As I have already stated in an earlier chapter, some people are also just more motivated than others, to do those mundane things like practice. This occurs because of a certain fire in their bellies that causes their minds to be positive and still creatively determined, as it affects their games. Desire and confidence do go hand and hand to make this game, a game of the mind as well as a game of the body. Many people stand on the 1st tee and their minds are filled with trying to remember sixteen things they feel they must do correctly to hit that first shot properly. When that happens we place our mind and mental state in a position to overload and maybe even to malfunction. It can even cause mental paralysis. There is a saying in golf that someone "cannot pull the trigger." In other words they cannot take the club away and then execute the shot because they are afraid of the consequence. We must front-load our minds with a few positive items, which will be the keys that allow us to approach this game in a positive and uplifting manner. If this does not happen we will not have fun, let alone play well. We should never forget that this is only a game. I have a couple of things I focus on when standing on that 1st tee. They are both golf-related and that is where I have to start. They have worked for me for a long time. They are mine and each person who plays this game needs to find their own points on which to focus.

On many occasions I have watched Fuzzy Zoeller walking down the fairway in the midst of a golf tournament and he most always looks as if he is out in a field somewhere walking and looking at the flowers and the birds. He seems to be whistling, chewing gum, and having a genuinely nice day. Do you think he is always as happy as he appears? He is probably not so all of the time. The whistling, most likely, calms him down and helps his mind to settle. That is the part of golf that is truly mental and the part that most people cannot lock into, merely because it is a hard connection to make, for the average person. The mind is often too fickle and too easily swayed from one place or thing to another, for it to hold on to any events of substance for any great length of time, as they relate to the game of golf. It does not take a genius to figure out that those players who can focus longer and better on certain areas of this game are going to be better at the mental part of this game than those who have limited focus. This is definitely true in those areas where their focus is good and solid. That should be obvious to most everyone. Then why do we have such a hard time focusing ourselves? The focus has to be on where you are at that moment and not where you have been or where you plan to go. Again let me say, each person who wants to play this game and wants to play it better has to find their own points on which to focus.

Being mentally tough is the level that separates the average player from the above-average player, when their physical skills are more or less the same. Sometimes the mentally tough player proves to be better than the less mentally tough player, even though the latter may be more skilled, with much more talent than the former. We must remember that "a little foolishness can out weigh a great deal of wisdom." Being emotional in a positive way allows the mind to focus on the situation at hand. That in turn allows the mind to maintain its direction and therefore gather and maintain some semblance of strength. If someone thinks they are strong enough to overlook little things that might cause the mind to wander, think again. Even the strongest of minds can fall prey to overconfidence and trips down memory lane and the fantasy freeway. If we think about something other than what our mission is when we are playing golf, then we have allowed our minds to wander. When this happens even those items that seem remote and even unimportant, like a piece of grass or a bug sitting on the ball before the tee shot is hit and the list goes on and on, become distractions. As was said before, invoking God's help in making a putt takes one's mind off of the putt itself. For that moment our concentration is broken and it may not return in that span of time. We have abandoned what we envisioned our mission to be: better golf and purer golf.

("A mind is a terrible thing to waste"…and allow to wander.)

It is important to strive toward a strong golf mentality. As we have mentioned already there is so much in this game that is purely mental. Every portion of this game that is positive requires the mind. There are no exceptions. There are golf mentalities and there are *golf mentalities*. Let me explain. I work as a chaplain in a medical center in San Francisco. Because of my amputation and my years of working with amputees, there are times when I am called upon to deal with people who have either lost their leg or are going to lose their leg, for various medical reasons.

On one occasion I was asked by a physician in the hospital to speak with a gentleman who had been brought into the hospital to have his leg removed because there was no circulation whatsoever in that particular limb. I saw him early in the morning on the day of his vascular surgery. We talked together and over and over again he explained to me that he was a golfer and that losing his leg was going to totally ruin his life. He was sure that his golfing days were completely finished. I explained to him that I was also a golfer and that I was sure he would be all right because the doctors would have him back out playing golf after his surgery and his adjustment to his new prosthesis. He said to me, "But you do not understand, I'm going to lose my leg and I am a 10 handicapper."

Finally I sat down beside his bed, pulled my pant's leg up, took my leg off, and held it up for him to see. When I did his eyes opened wide. I merely mentioned to him that I was a 4-handicap golfer. I put my leg back on and we talked a bit more. I left the room, knowing full well that he would watch me closely as I walked away. Later that day, after his surgery was finished and he was in the recovery room, I visited him once again. As he was waking up from his anesthesia he looked at me and I inquired if he remembered who I was. "Oh yes," he said, "you are the 4 handicapper." He did not mention my name or my profession, but he remembered that I was a golfer and that was the item that was foremost in his mind. That is *golf mentality*.

Someone once said that twenty percent of this game is physical and eighty percent of it is mental. This may or may not be true, but the fact remains that the player with the most toys at the end of a golf match is not always going to be the winner. The same could also be said about players with the most talent. Most of the time the player who is mentally stronger will win because he or she will make fewer mistakes, better shots, better choices and have lower scores. Those are the proper ingredients for victory. For instance just take the idea of thinking about asking God to invoke a bit of magic into a swing or a putt. I am sure that approach might help us mentally and spiritually, but it will not help us in the truest aspect of the golf game, as I alluded to earlier. The reason this is true is because we are thinking about something else instead of the aforementioned swing or the 4-foot putt. We most likely—no, we most definitely—cannot accept yet another distraction in our quest for an accomplished golf game. This is a game, yes and a mental one at that. Arnold Palmer once said, "What some people find in poetry, I find in the flight of a good drive." There is something profound in that statement. It is as if golf and all of the aspects of it were and are music to his ears. No one would ever dispute that he was a fine-tuned artist in this game of golf for oh so many years. (Thank you, Arnie.)

All people react mentally differently to things that come up in their golf life. Some show their anger outright while others, like Fuzzy Zoeller, appear calm on the outside. Yet only they know what is happening to them, on the inside. What they do with all of that emotion at that point is what really and truly matters. Some people talk to themselves and say things like, "good shot," or "you dummy," or various and sorted positive and negative declarations, and sometimes just nasty things in general. All of these expressions are how that person tries to deal with what is going on inside of them. All of these expressions do show exactly how a person feels inside.

When I worked at the Masters Golf Championship, I noticed one player who every time there was a backup on any teebox he would reach into his pants pocket and pull out a small picture holder. He would place the small square picture holder up to his right eye, point it toward the sun, and then after looking at it for a brief time, he would remove it from his eye, smile, and return it to his pants pocket. One time he caught me looking at him as he was replacing the small blue and white photo viewer into his pocket and he motioned for me to come to where he was sitting. "Do you want to see my picture, Son?" he asked. I shook my head no, feeling just a bit embarrassed. He gave it to me and encouraged me to look at the picture. I put it up to my eye, pointed it toward the sun, as he had done a few tmes that day, and what I saw has had a lasting effect on me, as far as golf was concerned. There was no picture in that tube, just four letters, K.I.S.S. I knew what they meant because they are the key to dealing with people and the key to being a good public speaker, as I was hoping to become with my studying at Emory University. For him it was the key to a great golf game. K.I.S.S. Keep it simple, stupid. That is how he dealt with his mental approach to this game. He used tools to remind him of the basics in his golf game. That is *golf mentality*.

When we think of *golf mentality* we need to think of swing thoughts. Often, as I mentioned earlier, we tend to have too many of them and that makes our minds so bulky and jumbled up that what is going on in our minds is doing us far more harm than good. We need to have some basic swing thoughts and patterns to get ourselves in a position to be ready to hit the golf ball and not be afraid to do so. We do not need sixteen thoughts as we address the golf ball. We also do not need cerebral automation. Confidence in our golf swings and confidence in our physical and mental capabilities are important. Remember the example of reaching for an old golf ball to hit across the water hazard or over a large barranca? There is no confidence in that act whatsoever. If we are going to be successful at this sport, then we have to want to be successful and we are going to have to believe that we can be successful. Without confidence there is no chance for sustained and true success in anything we attempt to do and that of course includes this great and wonderful game. This is not true if your view of success, as it relates to golf, is to go out and use the three or four hours or more on the golf course as an escape from your personal environment. Because if that is the case for you, if that is what you need, then your success is not to be found in golf perfection, but rather in easing your tormented mind. That, I can truly say, can happen with golf no matter what you intend to get from it, as far as expertise is concerned.

As a person with a disability, I have overcome some obstacles, but when I look around me there are people who are far worse off than I am—or ever was, for that matter. Some of them have no visible physical disabilities, only physical and mental limitations. There are people who are playing golf, as I write these words, who have no legs or no arms, people who are paralyzed and even blind, who are playing this game and playing it well, I might add. They love this game and they respect the game and they continue to play it no matter what comes upon them. You seldom ever here them complain, at least above a loud "Oh no" on occasions. The reasons for this are simple. They are playing golf, no matter how great or insignificant their games might be. That was not always a certainty for them. They have learned many valuable lessons through their life experiences and because of those experiences. Quite often they are emotionally stronger and many times more mentally aware, and that can give them an edge in the battle of golf achievements. If they do actually have that edge, it is because they understand what it truly means to really want to play the game of golf.

Once on a trip from North Carolina back to California following my mother's death, I decided to drive up to Canada and across to the west coast. It was late August and the weather was simply beautiful. I stopped along the way driving north to play golf here and there. In the western part of New York State I stopped in the little town of Lockport. I registered at one of the local hotels just off of the highway and got a good night's sleep. The following morning found me searching in the phone book for the addresses and telephone numbers of the local golf courses. Actually I probably did that before I did anything else.

Before long I was walking into the pro shop at one of those golf courses. The golf course was an old one, built back when golf courses did not have to be so gigantically long. When I entered the door of the pro shop there was a man sitting behind the counter of the shop. I spoke to him and introduced myself as I looked around the pro shop and into the glass case, which was filled with all kinds of golf balls and golf gloves. When he looked at me, it was as if he had seen a ghost. "You are from California, aren't you?" he asked and I was shocked, but readily admitted to the charge. Then he continued, "I am reading a story about you here in an old *Golf Digest* magazine. Wow." All I could say was the same thing. He showed me the article he had been reading from an issue of a publication that had been printed many months earlier. You talk about spooky… I asked him if I could play golf there and he was more than helpful to me in accomplishing that mission. The interesting part about Lloyd was that when he got up from the tall stool on which he had been sitting, he had only one leg.

Well—wow! I stayed there in the upper western corner of New York State for a few days and played golf every day with Lloyd, who was a 12 handicapper, and he played a good game of golf and on only one leg. He used no artificial limb at all. I was amazed at how well he hit the golf ball standing on just that one foot. He had such great balance. He really loved this game. One day he got us a game with a local judge and a good amateur player, and in the morning round they were beaten rather soundly. I happened to be in the restroom when our two opponents came into wash their hands after the morning round of golf. I was in one of the stalls and heard them say in disgust, "Can you believe that we got beat by two gimps?" I had raised my feet up off of the tile floor, to not give away my presence in the stall and my knowledge of their disdain. After they left the restroom I found Lloyd in the grillroom and I told him what had transpired in the men's room. He got up and crutched over to where they were standing, put his stump on his crutch and started talking fast and loud to them. When he came back to where I was sitting he said to me, "Get your clubs, preacher. They want to play us again. Are you ready?" He knew I was. On the 1st tee, after they had hit their shots, he leaned over to me with a gleam in his eye and a cigarette hanging limply out of the left side of his mouth and said, "Let's kick their asses." We were mentally ready, better in our heads than they were in theirs and we were not angry about being beaten by two gimps. Mission accomplished...

In July 1998 I was invited by a close friend of a friend of mine to play a wonderful golf course on the East Coast. I did not know anything about the person with whom I was scheduled to play golf except he seemed to be a nice person on the telephone.

When we got together at his golf course, I found out he was totally paralyzed from the waist down. Did he want anything special? Yes, you can bet he did. He wanted to play golf and golf to him was special. We did play golf and I will never forget how he stood alongside the golf cart and braced himself against one crutch with the support of two large braces, one on each of his legs. He took a good swing at the golf ball. By the way he was using only one hand. I know people who would ask why does a person go through all of that work just to play golf? He goes through it because he loves this game and because he has *golf mentality*. That is what this is all about. Loving this game. That is what it is all about. By the way Ed shot 83 and he just knew he should have done better. I think Ed has *golf mentality*.

Our attitudes and our emotions both are important because they can turn our golf games either sweet or sour. The same is true in all aspects of our lives. The object in the game of golf is to win, but winning is as much about what this game brings to us as far as sights, sounds, and feelings are concerned, as are our scores. When we come to realize this, our entire game will be better because our perspectives are different and even more defined. The feeling aspect of this game is where the Grace of this game is born.

If this sounds religious, I apologize because I wanted it to sound spiritual. It was said of Ben Hogan that practicing his golf game was an unnamed religious experience for him. I understand how that could be. It most likely placed him on a level, a special level of inner peace. That level was a sanctuary for him. That is what spirituality is supposed to do. It is supposed to make us special and yet normal. Our mentality, our attitudes, and our levels of peace have to be foremost in our relationship to golf for the package to be complete.

When we come to some sort of conclusion about ourselves and our relationship with golf and we look at what golf can do for us and to us, if we truly allow those things to happen, we will come to understand that there are a great number of elements that are in our lives because of golf. Some of those are bad, but for most people, most of these things are good things. I cannot think of but a few things in my mind that are negative because of golf. One of those is I need more time to play golf. I also feel bad sometimes that I feel so good about golf and some people do not have that same joy in their lives, golfers and non-golfers alike. I guess I cannot have it all.

Think for one minute of some of the things that golf gives to us. It gives us scenery, friendship, fellowship, clean air (most places), exercise (mental and physical), travel, emotional highs and lows (both of those are good things). I think of the old Hawaiian proverb that says, "There are no rainbows without the rain." We would and could not give the highs, in this game, their just dues without acknowledging the lows this game also grants us. We are given laughter, sunshine, all kinds of terrain, the challenge of self against nature and the course, and the list goes on and on. Still the one item golf allows us to have that minimizes all of the rest of the gifts given to us by golf, is peace. I can be alone or not on a golf course somewhere, literally anywhere, and I can feel a closeness to God that is only rivaled by some other spiritual experience. I guess that in some cases golf cannot rival itself, because there are times when this game can be a significantly spiritual experience, within itself. The reality is that this only happens sometimes, because at other times outside elements, such as other people (though they do not necessarily keep it away), the weather, or time restraints do not allow that level of peace to happen or to be attained. Yet when it happens I could hold it with me until it happens again somewhere down the road, on another grassy spot, under a sun-filled sky.

Yes, peace is what golf brings to me more than anything else in this wonderful game. Golf can grant us peace when there are so many things in our lives ready to rob us of that tranquility. In 1998 I was fortunate enough to play in the British Senior Amateur in the Troon and Prestwick area of Scotland. It was truly nice to be back in the land of my first golf odyssey. I arrived in Scotland early enough to practice for two days before the event began. My mind was a boiling cauldron of emotions as I drove toward the western coast of Scotland from Manchester, England. I arrived at the Glasgow Golf Course about 6:30 P.M., took my golf clubs out of the rental car, and started walking along the links of what was to be one of the venues for the tournament. The Glasgow Golf Club was quiet on that late afternoon as I walked along the first few holes. By the time I had reached the 5th and 6th holes I realized that it was only God, golf, and me out there. The wind was not to be felt, the gray clouds were puffy, and I felt finally at peace with all of the issues that had caused my mind and heart to be so busy in the past few days and weeks. I was once again blessed and truly at peace. Another time when peace came in the midst of turmoil because of two great loves.

There are times in my life when tears come to my eyes because of how humble I feel in many aspects of my life and in the relationship I have with golf. I am so blessed to be at peace with myself and with this great game. Sometimes I try to hold back the tears; but more times than not, it is of no use. I recall reading some of the early pages of this book to my dearest friend and some of his family and as I proceeded, the tears came freely from my eyes. Why? Very simply because I love this game and what it has done for me and to me. I feel special things because of where it has taken me, physically, mentally, and spiritually. The tears came to my eyes also because I feel special toward the friends with whom I was sharing some of these pages and because of where golf has taken us together. Some things are indeed in our lives and are attached to our souls. Those things are special to me because of their purity. So it is with this great game. It is indeed attached to my soul. That I feel is *golf mentality*.

In June of 1998 I was playing golf with some dear friends in North Carolina. After Ray, Mike, and I had finished our 18 holes,

I decided that I would like to go back out and play a few more holes, because the day was young and the mind and heart were on fire and strong. So I played another 6 or 7 holes alone. As I was approaching the last of those holes I noticed a tall younger man standing on the right side on the 18th green as I was putting out. As I walked off the green he said to me, "You do not remember me, do you?" Strangely enough I did know who he was. He and his family had been friends of mine many years before when I was a pastor in the city of Goldsboro.

He continued, "I do not know whether to hug you or to strangle you." I looked a bit perplexed and he once again continued and cleared up my confusion. "You got me started in this game thirty-two years ago and I am hooked." It was at that moment that we embraced. Tears, emotions, this game grants us all of those things if we are open to have them come into our lives. Once we reached the clubhouse I suggested that we go play a few holes together. He said, "Are you sure?" And my answer said it all, "Right," and off we went. He had 5 birdies in 12 holes. "This is amazing," he said, "first to be here with you after all of these years, and to have more birdies than I have ever had in even 18 holes." I was not surprised at either the birdies or the feelings, because they are only some of the things this game graces us with continually if we are open for that to come into our lives. That is what separates golf from all other sports. There are times in our golf lives that can be sheer magic and that afternoon in North Carolina, thirty-two years after the fact, was one of those times for two grown men on a golf course in Wayne County, North Carolina.

After we finished our few holes of golf, he drove me over to the home of my other friends, where I was staying. I retrieved my golf clubs from the back of his truck. I hugged him once again and he said, "Thank you again for getting me started and introducing me to this game." Wow, that is what it does to us. It makes us humble and grateful and grants us a tear or two at the right time. Golf is a mental and physical game, but it can be a game of the heart and a game of peace. We just have to be open for those things to happen in our lives and understand that they can come into our lives through the medium of golf.

Thank you, K. D., wherever you are for this gift in my life...

The mind is such an easy place in which to hide
And such a wonderful place to ride the wild fire.
It often frees us, but sometimes it cuffs us,
And we are different every time it changes,
Because of all of the places it will take us.

— CHAPTER SEVENTEEN —

The Metaphysical Visitations

It seems sometimes in life as we watch things unfold, that those things and events could be labeled the actions of a force far greater and beyond that of mortal men. Whether that is the case or not is still under study and consideration, at least for me. There are times in certain people's lives, (let's talk about golf here) when they could be justified for saying that an event or even a round of golf could have been the work of not only the person involved, but also an outside force. We have come to label some of those actions as deeds of the metaphysical world. We as humans are often ready to give the credit for some action or event of a special nature over to an outside force without taking into consideration one's own skills and the ever present possibility that sheer luck just might have been involved.

The hole in one that I mentioned earlier that occurred on the par 3 hole where I had scattered the ashes of a friend just two days before, is one of those events that might easily be considered as a visitation of the metaphysical. I am perfectly comfortable with that. I am also comfortable with the fact that I walked into a golf shop in western New York State, many miles away from my home in California, and the person there in the pro shop was reading an article about me from a magazine that was months old. That could well have been a mere coincidence, but it could have been more than mere coincidence also. Still it really seems to me that the forces that make up the metaphysical level of the universe would normally be too busy to just be dropping in and out of our lives and allowing things to happen to us here and there in some helter-skelter fashion.

Maybe these events happen because we want them to happen. Maybe they happen because we help them happen. I do not want to imply that I have all of the answers to these types of questions, nor do I need to have those answers. Still I do believe that if those events happen in our lives we need to just label them as blessed events because often they are without equal in many ways. The truth of the matter is that these events and times can and do occur in our lives, and no matter what we do they still might occur. I guess for me their origin is of little importance, but the fact that they did and do occur is of major importance to me.

I truly believe that golf shots are not made or directed by forces outside this realm. It seems sometimes there are people who have a great amount of luck, as it relates to a number of things in golf, while others seem to have less. You notice that I said less, as it relates to luck, because we are all lucky to be playing this game. I do believe that there are certain people who seemingly have more than their share of luck. They believe they will have good fortune and good bounces and many times that helps the process to happen. Those people who hit shots in the direction of the hole will make more aces than those who do not happen to have the good fortune of good direction. That is an easy equation to figure out. The famous shot hit on the 18 hole at the Old Course at St. Andrews to send the two players, one of which was John Daly, into a playoff for the British Open title could have been a shot of great skill or a shot of great fortune. I feel that to give rise to the idea that such a shot was the work of the metaphysical is nearsightedness, to say the least. It was indeed a shot of great fortune.

Tom Watson's famous shot on the 17 hole at Pebble Beach was a shot of great character and skill, but one of his own doing.

There was no particular reason or connection in either of these cases to invoke the metaphysical or give the metaphysical level of consciousness credit for either of those events occurring. There has to be a connection or a direct correlation to have that kind of event happen or be revealed. There are no special credentials one needs to have mortal visitations, just openness. These things happen a lot, but I am more than sure they are not always recognized for what they really are.

If there are metaphysical forces out there causing events and phenomena to happen they certainly are not going to announce themselves and show their presence to everyone who is standing around. I certainly have to believe they are far too busy to be doing self-investing campaigning. If these types of experiences are to come to us, all we have to do is to be ready to accept them if and when they do, and be grateful that they came to us and visited in our lives, to say nothing of our golf games.

I have to admit there are times when events in our lives seem somewhat unnatural. There are times when events seem more than a coincidence. In those times we have to just accept the reality of the event and feel good and blessed that it happened in our lives or we could wonder like an idiot, why it does not happen to us more often than it does. In some cases I am sure there is no thought processing at all, because many people never remember to count their many good fortunes. Of course human nature is weird, because when good things happen in many people's lives they continue to think those events will always happen without any help from themselves in the whole process. Good fortune, in golf, is like the good fortune we have with our families, our work, and our health. If we choose to believe that strokes of good luck will always be in our families, our health, our play, and our work they might just be there.

I mentioned in an earlier chapter about people who see their golf shots before they happen and then when the actual shot is hit, it seems to be a duplication of the shot already seen in their mind's eye. That is one of those items or events that seems difficult to explain or rationalize. You see, willpower plays a large

part in accomplishing those kinds of mental and even metaphysical events and levels.

Most people do not feel or think deep enough or hard enough
to allow those wonders to materialize and/or to occur in their
lives. We have to be open to allow those chances and times to
visit us. There is nothing dark and sinister about this whole process. There is nothing eerie at all in the approach to this emotional
and spiritual plane or some other level somewhere else. The
rule here is to understand that these events happen with or without our help or recognition, but when they happen, if they are
perceived as dark and negative, then that is how we will forever
label them. They are only dark if that is what we think they are.
For the most part there is no need to try and rationalize why
they happen or how they happened. Just relax and enjoy what
at times can feel like magic in our lives and in our golf games.
When something wonderful happens it may be skill or a stroke
of good fortune or even a visitation. The reality is, whatever it is,
whether we can pin down the source or not, it does not matter.
Just feel blessed. I am sure that you are.

Please understand that those events in golf that might be
construed or even misconstrued as from some metaphysical plane
somewhere do not come by choice. If we are fortunate enough
to recognize them in our lives, we have to be ready, willing, and
able to accept them. We have to be open and strong enough to
think on that sometimes farfetched level. On the other hand if
we recognize them, then we might be ready to be open and
accepting of those farfetched ideas.

There are times in one's life—I speak from my own experience of course—when occurrences seem almost as if they are
supernatural or even divine in their nature or genesis. That could
well be because that is how we view them and their worth for
us. There is no doubt in my mind that God has had a hand in the
events in both my life and my golf. I know that because both of
them have been deeper, far more spiritual, and more bound together than a coincidence could ever have caused them to be.
All I have been able to say is "Thank you," and more times than
I can begin to remember. I do have to try and remember Carl

Sagan's words though, that "The universe forces those who live in it to understand it." So it is with this game, its roots, its emotions, and its parallel trek with the spiritual side of life, my life in particular. In all of those aspects of life there are lessons to be learned. Mostly the universe and those lessons force us to understand ourselves more and more, or maybe not. The lessons in life are only lessons and they are only valuable if we grow and learn from each of them.

In Chapter Four, I wrote about my trip to Vietnam and I mentioned that the young soldier who was assigned to me as a chaplain's assistant was named Gary Palmer. I found that to be quite interesting especially since, as I mentioned also in that same chapter, two of the most prominent players in those days in the world of golf were Arnold Palmer and Gary Player. I do not believe something like this is as much coincidence as it is providence. I try to understand the universe and how it turns and relates to my world, and I also really try to appreciate it. Still having that knowledge of myself I will always be a bit unsure of the coincidences and bits of providence in this issue, as well as so many others that have happened to me.

Golf has no roots, for me, in the occult. There are people who believe that such a notion might be the truth or even in vogue, but it is not for me to believe. The whole idea of the occult pulls up visions of darkness and deep holes on the black side of the metaphysical experience and sphere in this life and that other life out there somewhere. To start with, golf is a product of the light, of the mind, of the heart, of the good pure spirit, and of perfection. It can bring to our attention realities that might well happen for a reason, not just by luck or by coincidence, but by an intervention. Still having said that, we must always remember that golf gives to us many things, but for me not one of those things is negative or is conceived in the occult.

If we view golf as if there are demons in the game then those demons will make themselves known to us one way or another in the game, because we put them there and we have given them their life. Most people do have some demons in their golf lives merely because they place them there. Remember, those demons have life only if we give them life. Those demons most likely are what we see when we look in the mirror in the morning to shave or to comb our hair.

The only magic in golf is not the black magic type. It is the good kind of magic that comes from just truly enjoying a time of peace on a beautiful piece of God's earth, a warm day, a friendly breeze, beautiful skies, wonderful solitude, or the joy of fellowship with a good friend or two. That is the real and sheer magic that this game can bring to us and that is neither dark, diminished, or demonic.

All of the various things that can happen to us as we play this game, can happen when we are alone, absolutely without pressure on us to play well, or those same things can happen to us when we are with friends, or they can happen to us in front of large crowds of strangers. That is another powerful part of the magic woven by this game of the non-occult. We talked a bit earlier about holes in one and how they seem to be a part of some people's lives more than others. There was a professional mentioned in an earlier chapter who at last count had made more than 50 holes in one. There is nothing mystic about that. I am sure that many people would disagree with this statement, but he hits the ball at the target and when that happens occasionally one of those shots will find the bottom of the cup. If he were here right now talking to me he would tell me, as he has stated before, that he has made so many holes in one merely because he was lucky and because he hit the ball in the correct and proper direction. He would also tell me that he was lucky because he began to play this game many, many years ago. I know a bit about how that feels.

If you believe there are forces out there reading your putts and causing your ball to do wonderful and/or weird things, then you depend on a undependable source for your golf game's success. Oh, I believe there are forces in our midst and in all the areas and aspects of our lives. I have been made aware of their presence in more places than just the golf course. I do believe that when Ben Crenshaw won the Master Golf Championship, soon after the death of his mentor, friend, and coach, that there was an aura around him in the image of Harvey Pinnick. I also believe that he felt that presence strongly and it caused him to believe in himself and to remember many of the great bits of wisdom passed along to him by his teacher and friend. He was able to stay focused in that time and place because the fueling of his mentor was in his heart and mind and not just a part of his physical strength, his swing, and memory past.

The same experience, yet different in some ways, was there for Davis Love the Third when he won that memorable PGA Championship. No one who witnessed the happenings of that day will ever be able to forget how he stood there on that last green with tears streaming down from his eyes as that beautifully colored giant rainbow encircled him, as if to give him comfort. We all knew he was thinking about his father and all of the times they had spent together grooming him for that time and that place in his life. I believe that is how the metaphysical really works. There are no black shadows crossing a green causing some strange experience to happen. Those visitations do not cause golf shots to turn in the air and fall short of the target or go right or left of the target. Metaphysics, whatever their makeup might be, are far too busy for all of that triviality. It is not that those shots are trivial to the person who strikes them, but in the full course of life itself and the events of life, they are small items, insignificant to the world events around us. They shine dimly as they relate to the rest of the whole of golfdom.

Yes, there are memories and there are images that can flood our mental space relative to golf, both good and bad, but they are only there at our invitation or behest. We open the mental door and they come crashing in, causing good things and bad things to pass our way. When the bad bounces occur it is easy for us to once again take our mind off of our intended goal and mission. When the mind strays into a deep negative canyon somewhere, it will pull us in with it more times than not. Those journeys are not caused by the metaphysical, but rather they are a result of weak-mindedness. They are the result of someone who has forgotten so quickly the good bounce that occurred only a few moments earlier. Those journeys belong to the average person who plays at this above-average game we lovingly call golf.

I believe in the metaphysical side of this game, just as I believe that it is in my life, but I see it being somewhat elusive as to its involvement with everyone who plays this game. I feel that we cannot allow it to control us and if it does, like so many other things, it will do just that. I believe the putt I eluded to, that happened at the Whitemarsh Country Club in the presence of all of those Vietnam veterans sitting in their wheelchairs, was motivated by my desire to be a positive force for them as they watched all of that unfold. Was an outside force present? Of course there was. It was there because I invited it in; I wanted that help and that presence, and I was open for it to happen. Gene Sarazen was open for the great double eagle shot at Augusta National to happen. It might have been just a miracle, but the reality is that it did happen.

That is truly all that matters. The shot that was hit onto the 18th green to tie John Daly in the British Open was a shot that might have had help, other than luck, but the reality is that it happened and that's all that really matters. People can be ready to have a miracle happen in their lives and many times that miracle occurs. My being given a chance to feel these kinds of visitations allows me to be on the same level with other golfers, great and small, as far as talent goes. That is how golf treats us. Pretty nice, huh?

The metaphysical is real and as I stated earlier, it is in my life and in all aspects of my life. Still it is not a dark shadow, but rather a helping hand. I have had 2 rounds of golf in my life where I shot 62. They were both different. One was clean and crisp and the other was iffy, to say the least. I could not have hit the golf ball any better than I did in the pure round and I have never had a round where I hit so many balls off of trees and chipped other shots into the hole as I did in the less than crisp round. Someone playing with me said, "God is sure watching over you." In both rounds that was the comment. They were both right, but there was no metaphysical visitation, except as it is always present in my life. That presence is there because I welcome it in. That presence pushes me to the driving range and to the putting green. That presence is good and positive and that presence would not do anything to me that is negative. That is what the metaphysical is all about in my life.

If we view the metaphysical as dark and sinister, then it will be just that for anyone who perceives it in that fashion. I have no room in my life for that dark cloud of negativity. Golf is a child of the light and that means it is positive. So there....

Visitations come to us all,
At times known to us and not so.
Filled with thoughts and feelings
Of different matters and strengths.
Yet we manage to survive,
Many times totally unaware of their presence.

CHAPTER EIGHTEEN

The United States Senior Open

I have heard it said there are special times in most everyone's life that seem to be sheer magic. In 1994 in the northeastern corner of South Carolina at a golf course by the name of Long Bay (one of Jack Nicklaus' designs) I, like so many others in various sections of the country, endeavored to fulfill a dream. It was a hot and humid July day and the presence of the sun made the heat that much more intense. I was trying for the second time in two years to qualify for the United States Senior Open Golf Championship. I had also tried to qualify the year before but I had fallen two shots short of that goal.

I realized I was only one of thousands who were also trying to fulfill a dream of playing golf with those professionals, whom we have watched and sometimes admired on the pro golf tour for many years. At least that is how I felt. Many of the players who would play in that Open Championship were men who brought golf into my awareness and who came from the era when I was just starting to play this wonderful game. Their names, to this day, still foster thrill after thrill as those remembrances are pulled up from my memory bank. I wanted to walk at least once in that company of this game's great elder giants. Alas, so did all of the others around this country with that same ambition and that same dream.

After hitting a number of practice shots and putting for an extended period of time I made my way to the 1st tee, a few minutes ahead of my scheduled tee time. Before I had hit even one shot on that day good things began to happen. I was joined on the 1st tee by the other two competitors in that day's threesome of would-be qualifiers. One of those two players was a man I had not seen in twenty-seven years. He and I had been in the army together at Fort Bragg, North Carolina, before I had been sent to Vietnam.

This former sergeant in the military was now a golf professional and living in that part of South Carolina. After all of the introductions were complete I stood over to the side of the teebox, awaiting my turn to hit that 1st tee shot, thinking just how amazing it was that two men who had not heard about or seen each other in so many years, could meet there in that special time and that extremely remote place. I will remember that day and I will remember the warm embrace that passed between two men whose paths crossed finally after all of those years. It happened on the golf course, where else? We both asked almost at the same time, "What are the chances, with more than a one hundred players here today, that we would be paired together in the same group?" One might say that it was the luck of the draw, but I figured it differently.

I will not belabor the point with a hole-by-hole remembering of my round. I will only say that I shot even par. That was good enough to tie for second place with two other players. One other player, the medalist, had shot a subpar round and therefore had automatically qualified for the upcoming championship in Pinehurst. There were three spots allowed to the qualifiers. That meant there had to be a playoff for the other two spots.

I could draw this out, but I refuse to put myself through that again. I lost in the playoff, but I thought I had played my best. I had walked 20 holes in the ninety-plus degree weather and I had shot even par. Of course I was disappointed to not qualify for the Open and as I drove to my daughter's home that afternoon, I kept thinking, "All I can do is keep trying." I knew I had been so close, but I was still so far from that special dream. I was deemed an alternate and I knew that alternates hardly ever made the Big Game. "Maybe one day my chance would come," I thought out loud to myself, because that has always been my approach. "I will just keep at it until something else good happens and in this game; it always seems to." I was probably talking out loud to myself more than merely thinking, as I drove north and west.

I arrived back in California the following day and of course I went back to work. Many of my friends from the hospital where I work, and from the golf course where I play most of my golf, called to inquire as to how the qualifying had gone and I told the story over and over and over again. It was never easy to tell how I lost in a playoff, no matter how many times I had to tell the story, but I realized that few people or teams even make it to the playoffs.

The next day I received a phone call from the USGA informing me that as an alternate I had been selected to play in the Open to fill a spot vacated by a player with some physical problems. He had sustained a foot injury. Of course, the player with the injured foot was replaced by an amputee. The irony of that scenario was overwhelming to me. I laughed to think, "That is how it should be." I could not remember all of the details of the phone conversation because I was rather excited, to say the least. I recall going into my supervisor's office at the hospital where I worked, who just happened to be one of my best golfing friends. I looked somewhat sad and explained to him that I needed to use some of my vacation time. He looked rather concerned, as a good friend would naturally be when they see another friend looking a bit down. "Are you all right? Can I do anything?" Then I told him what had happened and he just jumped with joy and came over and hugged me. That is what friends do. They are happy when we are happy. Two days later I left for North Carolina, Pinehurst, and the United States Senior Open.

The weather was the same as it always is, in the middle of summer in that part of North Carolina. It was hot and humid with rain on and off and of course in that tournament there were no golf carts, so everyone walked. It only took the day of the practice round for me walking the golf course in the heat, the humidity, and with a poorly fit artificial limb to totally destroy my stump. I shot seventy-six in the practice round and was happy. That is except for the condition of my leg.

On the first day of the tournament I was paired with two well-known senior golf professionals. In the first 2 rounds of the tournament I did not play well at all for all of the reasons I have already mentioned above. In those two days of play, I literally played 2 of the worst rounds of golf I had ever played in my life, or at least in the last twenty-five years of my life—in my entire memory for that matter. Yet in all of that physical and emotional pain some wonderful things did happen. When I finally finished the struggles of the first day, I was glad it was over and disappointed in how I had played. Some of my faithful friends had been nice enough to follow me for the full 18 holes on that first day and I am sure they labored on every shot with me, as I fought my way around that great old golf course.

When the round was over and I was walking off the 18th green a young boy in a wheelchair, who was being pushed by his father, came over and asked me for my autograph. I was so touched because his father had pushed him for my last 9 holes in that heat, to watch such an awful display of golf. I had noticed the two of them earlier in the round. I guess the score did not matter much to them. I was so deeply moved by him being there that I was only a short distance from tears. This game will do that to us.

That evening all I could do was sit in a tub of hot water and soak my leg and try to figure out how I was going to walk the next 18 holes on the following day. I do not want to give anyone the impression that I was some kind of hero or martyr, but needless to say, I ate in my room that night and soaked in the tub for a long, long time. The following morning it was hard just to get my artificial leg on, but it was going on one way or another. I was going to make my tee time.

On that second day there were rain delays because there had been heavy rain storms in the area and several inches of water had fallen in the night and in the early morning hours. The rain had literally soaked the fairways. When we finally did get a chance to play, everything was extremely wet including my golf scores. Still the wheelchair was there again and an occasional round of applause from the gallery members who had seen poor golf from me, but also stern determination to keep on plugging along in spite of how poorly I was playing. I stopped several times during the round to change the liner in my prosthesis and to change the bandage that was on the open wound on my leg. When we finally reached the 18th hole I was tired, wet, sore and extremely embarrassed at the way I had played in this great championship. Yet there was a special joy inside of me from just being there, seeing the people, and hearing their comments of encouragement. That is indeed something else that golf does: it bonds people together in a single message, feeling, and cause.

The long par 4/18th was playing extremely long that day because the fairway was like a sponge from all of the rain and it was all uphill. I hit a driver off of the tee and then I hit a fairly good 4 wood. I still had about 90 yards to the middle of the green so I hit a pitching wedge within about 8 inches of the hole. When I limped onto the green the bleachers rose all together in applause. I remember thinking to myself, "Suppose I had played well?" I was overcome with emotion. I recalled watching golfers on television and in live tournaments come on to the final green of a tournament and the people give them a salute by rising. I guess that was mine for my life and I will never forget the warm chills that ran through my body as I walked over and tapped in that final putt. I believe that for me was a time to be labeled as sacred. I walked over to the edge of the green and waited for the other two players to putt out. As I looked around at the faces of all of those people in the gallery, I could not help but look a bit upward and give a word of thanks to God for that special moment in my life. My golf scores had been really bad, but the joy was prominent and most likely everlasting. I say the golf scores had been bad, because golf itself is never bad, at least for me.

As I write these words, the first so written about that event by me since it happened, I am still thankful for that time in my life. I am still filled with deep emotions about that final walk and the warm greetings from those understanding and kind people in the bleaches surrounding the south side of the 18th green. My wish would be that they could somehow know how good and excited they made me feel. I wish those good feelings for them, at least one time in each of their lives.

Later inside of the interview area I was surrounded by reporters. My daughter and my grandson were there on that second day and I just could not control my feelings of pride, pain, and some embarrassment. Then I looked over the crowd of photographers and there I saw the same young boy in his wheelchair smiling at me. I made my way through the group of people between where he was and where I was because I just felt the need to hug him. My emotions were at an ultimate level. I had photographs taken with the young man and his father. That was without a doubt one of the true highlights of that whole experience for me. That is one of the wonderful things that golf did for me, on that special day.

That evening I was lying in my hotel room thinking about the past few days. I thought my days at the Open were finished, but little did I know.

The following morning I went back to the golf course to clean out my locker. As I was walking toward my locker I passed the lockers bearing the names of all of the great players who had been there for the Open and I knew, down deep in my heart, that not one of them had felt any deeper about the whole experience of being there than I had. Then as I was leaving I passed through the clubhouse one more time going out toward my car and an elderly black gentleman, who worked there at the golf course said to me, "I hope you will come back to see us again. It was wonderful for me to get to know you. My son has a leg like yours. I told him about you." I felt happy about that vote of confidence.

I sat in my car, there in the parking lot and I remembered a couple of negative things that had happened in that short span of time and I realized they were really not important at all, in the total scope of what had happened in my life in those past three days. I felt a tear come to my eye and remembered once again what my dad had told me when I was a young boy and had come home crying about something. "It is not a sign of weakness to cry," he said, "but rather it is a sign of sensitivity and strength." Man I had been strong a lot that week…

A few days later I was back home in California. I received a number of telephone calls and telegrams from well-wishers, friends and strangers alike. There were messages from amputees and their families asking for various kinds of advice on how to get started playing golf and how to get better at playing this great game. I felt really moved, for that was one of the reasons that drove me to be there in Pinehurst in the first place, to be an example as to what people with disabilities can do if they set their minds to it. I received a letter from the little boy in the wheelchair thanking me for being there at Pinehurst and thanking me for giving him an autographed golf ball and again, well you know.

The only real exhibition of true skill I showed in the two days of play in that great golf tournament was on the par 4/5th hole which was a wet 430 yards. The hole was slightly uphill with a large ditch crossing the fairway, up in front of the green. Both days I hit a drive to the right side of the fairway. I proceeded at that point to lay up short of the ditch with a 4 wood on my second shot and then hit a pitching wedge onto the green. Then I one-putted for par. I did that both days and in our threesome I was the only player to make pars both days, on that particular hole. I mention this only because sometime following my return home, I received by mail a painting of that particular hole, nicely framed, from one of my golf friends who had been kind enough to follow me around those two days of would-be golf. It will remain hanging there on my wall, in case my mind goes completely blank and I need some help to remember something that I am most likely never going to forget while I am still breathing. Thank you, Joe, for keeping that memory alive for me.

There are so many different emotions running around in my head and my heart about those days and times at "the Open.." There were times and memories of the physical pain and mental frustration, but they are minute in comparison to the memories that bring tears to my heart and my eyes about that whole wonderful experience. This game has granted me so many levels of joy that it is quite difficult to bring them mentally up and write about them all. That sounds redundant, doesn't it? Redundant it is, but oh so true.

The U.S. Open was an experience I will always hold dear to my heart as a time I can truly say that I walked where the best in this game have walked. They are better than I am at this wonderful game, but I doubt that there is one out there who loves it anymore than I do. They would even be hard-pressed to love it as much as I do… I can say this with some sense of confidence. I may not be finished, we'll see….

On a passing note, when I registered for the Open, I had been given a locker right in the middle of some of the greatest names in golf. One day, as I was getting ready to go out and play one of my rounds, in walked one of the great professionals and a famous member of the Senior Golf Tour. I had known his father for years. I mentioned to him that I knew his father and he acted as if that was nice, in a remote sort of way. Then I lowered my pants to adjust my prosthesis before going out to play that particular round of golf. He looked at my leg and asked, "Are you the Preacher?" That is what his father had always called me. I admitted I was and I felt proud of the charge. All of a sudden he seemed different. The game and the spirit of it that watches over us. Wow!

Oh I must mention that in the letters and telegrams I received due to my being there in Pinehurst, there was one particular telegram that read as follows: "This is from a friend in the far distant past. I saw you today on television at the golf tournament in North Carolina and I must say, that you did Find A Way, to play golf again! God bless you Chaplain." It was signed "The Sarge." I remember reading those words and seeing his face, embossed in the yellow page of that telegram, looking down at me as I lay there on the jungle floor after I had stepped on that land mine just a few minutes before. I could see his face outlined by the thick jungle foliage and his stark expression, then so many years before. He was right; I guess I had found a way. His words were as clear in that telegram as they had been on that December day, back there in 1969. The Way taught me the way....

> *Gifts are precious things given to those we love.*
> *When they are given to us,*
> *We need to cherish both the gift and the giver,*
> *Understanding that they are given in love*
> *And we are most fortunate to have the gift,*
> *But more so to have the giver in our lives.*

— CHAPTER NINETEEN —

My Philosophy As It Relates to This Game

A person's philosophy or their philosophic approach to anything may be good for them and may fit or fulfill their own personal needs. Still the truth of the matter is, a person's philosophy may only be good for them and no one else. That is indeed all right because it is theirs and they can use it in their lives and for their lives only, unless they are called upon to share those feelings and opinions with other people. I guess philosophies are merely opinions; they are like backsides in that everybody has one. Some people may recognize their opinionatedness or they may not. Their philosophies may be good or bad in the eyes of outsiders, but that does matter as long as those opinions work for their beholder. The following pages are my opinions and my philosophies on this game of golf. They are my opinions and my thoughts and they have worked for me in the past—and certainly work for me in the present—and I foresee them doing the same in the future.

I do realize that people love this game so much for so many varied reasons. First of all, for many of us it (golf) has been with us longer than most of our relationships and many of our possessions. I have actually known golf longer than I have known my own daughter. I have had golf in my life longer than I knew my father, who died when I was only twenty years of age. Many who read this have had golf in their lives longer than they have had their wives or their husbands in their lives. It has lasted the test of time when other relationships have sometimes descended into ruin. Secondly, golf has filled our lives with hope, joy, and yes even love for a long, long time. It may be hard for some of us to remember when golf was not around and in our lives. There are times when golf may have few if any emotional equals in one's life. Be that good or bad, it is true in many situations. This is not always determined by how well ones plays the game of golf.

Golf is also the one constant inconsistency in our lives. It drives us toward perfection day after day, even though the wise man knows beyond a shadow of doubt that perfection is well out of the reach of most of us mortal men and women. Still the journey associated with the climb toward that level of perfection is many times overpowering and to say the least, thrilling. In most of our life's quest toward perfection in things such as work or relationships there might be a tendency to feel negative if we fail to attain that perfection. These feelings are often brought about because of all of the pressure surrounding the quest to achieve that place of near immortality.

In our golf quest the situation is different because we want to achieve certain goals and not just because we feel we have to do so. In golf there is an emotional attachment in our quest for perfection, whereas in other areas of our lives those striving for perfection are fueled by some other emotional or physical level, such as peer pressure or the ideas of social failure and/or economic disaster. The central pulse of import here is the whole idea of wanting to achieve certain goals because of an emotional relationship with the game of golf. Most of the other areas of our lives, where we are trying to achieve something special, are places where we feel we have to do so because of the things we face in our environment. We have to succeed or else, in most of those areas. Golf makes us want to succeed at it and not just feel that we have to do so or else.

Golf, as I have said over and over again, is only a game. If we attempt to change what golf is then we take away from the game the points that give it the power it has. That is definitely true yet the game of golf is more. Golf can be a relationship and one, as I stated earlier, that might well last longer than many human relationships in our lives will last. Golf, if taken correctly, can have a deep-rooted relationship to our hearts and our minds, as do religion, philosophy, and spirituality, as we noted earlier.

Not everyone can comprehend the spiritual side and level of this game. That is simple to understand when we look at just how their spiritual life is or is not, as the case may be. If one is not spiritual in their everyday life then they will find it more difficult to be spiritual, as far as the game of golf is concerned, than someone who has already made that connection. The simple truth is that many people do not even think about the spiritual aspects of this game. It is not something they have a need for merely because they have not yet walked in that Garden. To some this game is an exercise of wills and an exercise of the mind and body only. Too bad.

As we try to better understand this game and our great attraction to it, as well as our great need to be a part of it, we must embrace the reality that in golf there are no endings, just discoveries, just beginnings if you will. There are so many doors golf can open up for us. There are so many new beginnings out there, and one of those might well be trying to understand the spiritual aspects of this game of golf. If our relationship to this great sport is with an open mind, then many wonderful things can come our way. Adventures can be around every corner or every dogleg and even across every barranca. There are so many new and different ways to view the sunsets and the fast-moving cloud formations. There are truly wonderful rocks and trees with great and strange shapes that can translate wonderful images to our minds. There are indeed new discoveries literally around every bend in the fairway. We just have to be open to search for them or to just see them, for they are gifts out there just waiting to be seen, waiting for you and me to take advantage of them.

As I related earlier, I almost always feel a bit down when the 18th hole rolls around or when the 36th hole comes, if I am in one of those frequent thirty-six hole days of golf. The reason for this is quite simple: I just do not want to stop what I am doing, and that of course is playing golf and spending time with special friends. Sure there is darkness and there are rainstorms, but still neither of them quenches my desire to play this game. What else affects us (me) this way? Very little if anything. The same is true as it relates to my profession. I do not want to retire, but one day that will happen because of age and whatever else may be out there waiting. The same might be true with this game of golf. I might one day have to retire that A.J. Tech Shaft. I am desperately hoping that the time of retirement in both of these areas will not be simultaneous.

The reason I feel the way I do about this game is simple. It is the one thing in my life that causes me absolutely no pain whatsoever, other than an occasional physical one. I have no anguish, no lasting frustration, and I know that it will not give me ulcers, if I were prone to ulcers, which I am not. I can also look forward to playing golf again when a round is over, as soon as the next day, or even the same day if the days are long enough and the storms stay either north or south of where I am. I can look forward with great anticipation to all of those discoveries out there waiting for me on the round just ahead. The process of anticipation is great and most of the time the actual event, when it arrives, lives up to the anticipation itself.

Often we are confronted by people around us who seemingly do not understand how and why we can enjoy something as much as we seem to enjoy golf. It is easy and often quite understandable how we can get upset and exasperated with them. Yet we need to think long and hard about the situation before we do that, because there are reasons for them feeling the way they do. The main reason is simple. They have no way of understanding and/or no ability to focus on the places where golf can and has taken us, and the peace and joy it allows us in our lives. Many of them have never enjoyed the feeling level golf offers to us. They have never felt the competitive spirit golf can place in our lives. They have never felt the depth of companionship and friendship golf grants us when it is pure and pristine. Do not resent their tirades, but instead try to understand they are frustrated because of the lack of feelings, joy, and knowledge in their lives that golf brings to you.

Take into consideration that sometimes we as golfers are guilty, of spending more time at play than at home or other places. Maybe we need to help those around us who seem to begrudge us our time in the Garden—if that is what it is to you, as it is to me—to better understand our place of joy and peace. Maybe they could be a part of that space, maybe not. If they do not want to understand where this game takes us, then that is a different matter altogether.

Each and every person who has ever had a relationship with golf has experienced some perfect moments as they relate to golf. Those moments could be one or many, but the chances are good that they have occurred at some point in each golfer's life. That is the nature of the sport. That is what drives us to keep at this game when so many other things in our lives often fail. A simple chip shot, a long sought-after victory, over a special golf course or over part of one's mind, a walk with friends or alone, watching the clouds bubble up and move past us at the direction of the wind. There are holes in one, eagles, or the moment when a person realizes for the first time that the moment they were just granted was as near perfect as it could possibly be. It has happened to them because golf has happened to them.

Do you remember such a time? Maybe not, but it has been there. Quite often we just do not take the time to notice. Many times in my golf life, I have taken a bit of time in a round of golf to just thank God for a special moment just experienced by me, or by a friend who might have been with me. This goes beyond actions and deeds to space and place and one's position in both. Those perfect moments can and most probably will happen to anyone who has a positive relationship with this game of golf.

The amazing thing is that they will occur no matter what one's relationship to golf might be. That is the nature of the game of golf.

In this game of golf, as in the game of life, most people want to give a little and get a lot. There are always people around who want to get something for nothing. Our surroundings, if you will observe, are saturated with people asking for so many things that golf will only give to us if we give to it. That does not mean if someone wants to just take a walk on a golf course and hit the golf ball in whatever direction it happens to fly, that they will not receive something special from that time. They will indeed be blessed by the experience, if they are open to the benefits it can produce. What it does mean however, is that if someone is striving to be better and trying to reach for that elusive level or goal of perfection, as it relates to golf, they cannot achieve many steps in that directions without putting a great deal of work into the process.

The more we put into golf, the more we will receive from it. Most everything in life is the same way. Between being involved with golf and working hard to be better at it, moments of joy, surprise, and above all excellence will occur time and time again. The old adage: "A blind hog finds an acorn," may be true, but if you have a good work ethic, relative to this game, perfect moments will happen in more ways than just by blind off-the-wall luck. We must always remember that these moments are merely physical ones by nature if they just happen without the thought process that could and must accompany them.

We need to remember also that moments of excellence may occur often because one's mind is on fire with just the memory of one thing that might have happened. That event could seem trivial to many people, but mentally major to others. If someone tries to explain that moment of joy or that feeling of excellence to someone else it might well fall on deaf ears, merely because those who listen lack the interest to find our tales of excitement worthy of their time. They might not be able to understand our journey, merely because for them it might well be a road never traveled.

If someone can remember a special moment of excellence in their golf life, they must understand that is only one of the places where golf can take them. Golf can take us to beautiful places, both near and far. Still golf can take us to places of peace that no other sport can, because that is the epicentral nature of the game. This will only happen though if we are open for peace to come into our lives, relative to this game. It can and does happen in this game and for that, little travel is needed. Golf can also take you to places that are truly traumatic in nature, and in the moment before that thought is even finished it can grant you and me real joy. Still we have to allow all of this to happen. We need to be able to totally focus on what we are doing and that is not always easy. It is never easy to forget all of the negative things (the crap) in one's life and find a way to focus on the wonderful walk, alone or with friends, through our adventures with golf.

If golf does not grant you peace, it is not the fault of the game. Some people may not want peace from this game—for that matter they may not even think about that, relative to golf or anything else. That is too bad because it can be such a wonderful asset in everyone's life. It can center and solidify so many different parts of our lives.

I want to talk about focus for a brief moment here. It is so important to do so, because focus is important in everything we attempt to do. It is important in raising a family. It is important in pursuing a career, driving a car, or driving a golf ball. What focus does, if we apply it in the correct dosage, is make whatever we are involved in better and more intense. That can be good and bad. Still what we are thinking about here, relative to focus, is how that is associated with our golf game. Focus is of the utmost importance to anyone who would attempt to climb up that skill ladder in the game of golf. If that ladder is not important to you, then focus is something you can pass on, as far as golf in concerned.

It is no secret and it does not take a person with a PhD to figure out, that in one's golf life, we play better golf if we remain aware of what we are doing and where we are all of the time.

The same is true in driving a car and most, if not all, of the things we are involved in every day. Some people often play better golf if there is something at stake, a wager, a title, or even just bragging rights. The reason, in most cases, that they play better under those circumstances is basically simple: they remain more focused under those conditions than they normally do when they are out there just banging golf balls around the golf course by themselves. There are no mulligans when something is at stake. There are a number of items that can and often do bring us out of the shades of mediocrity, and focus is one of those things that will make us better because we will concentrate more and longer on whatever we are trying to do.

Take for example a simple golf shot. I am sure that we are all a bit guilty of doing this: when we approach a short easy hole or an easy shot we often fall into that deep mental trap of losing focus. We believe the hole or the shot is so easy that it takes no concentration to play the hole well or to make a good shot. Instead of making the proper shot and conquering the hole we thought was so easy with a birdie, we lose our focus and we lose the hole. The birdie, which was going to be so easy for us to make, just flies away. We fell into the trap of being overconfident, not believing that focus was necessary, and losing the hole because we were out of mental control.

More times than not if we approach those short par 3s, 4s, and 5s with a non-focused attitude we will totally mess those holes up with bogies or worse. How many times have we heard or said ourselves, "I just went to sleep" or "I had a brain lock or brain fade"? What these comments mean is simple and they are not complimentary. Translated they mean that the person lost his or her focus. Focus is important in life and golf both, if we are going to improve in those two areas in the weeks, months, and years ahead for us.

What separates the elite players in your golfing friendship circles from those who are even better than they are at this game, is truly skill. That skill is both physical and mental. That skill is nurtured with a great deal of patience and a great deal of practice. Still there are other buttons that can be pushed to help those players who are better than the good players to be even better. There are elements that help and hinder players of all levels in the pursuit of excellence in their golf games.

For instance, if I know that I am under some time restraints, it is better for me to practice my game rather than to try and play a round of golf. This is true because if I try to play when I have an appointment pending, I will be concerned about my time frame and the obligation that I have to take care of at the end of that period of time which I have allotted for golf. I find myself hurrying shots as if to get them over with so I can make my next meeting. When we play golf in a rush we often play golf poorly. By doing this we have created yet another mental hurdle over which we must climb the next time we go out to play golf. We often ask ourselves over and over again, "Why did I play so badly last week?" Therefore our games will suffer as a result of this mental squeezing of time that is going on inside of us.

If a person feels that his or her world is in turmoil it will often carry over into their golf game. That is merely human nature. All of the outside stuff in our world can carry over and become encased in our hearts and heads and affect everything we do. That of course includes golf. When our heads are filled with matters that seem to complicate our lives then we are in a dark valley and totally out of focus. We become one with something other than golf, be that good or bad.

A person's mind-set is far more important than most people will ever understand. When we pick up the newspaper on Monday morning and turn to the sports section and there search for, find, and read about the person who won the latest golf championship over the weekend, you may well rest assured that the winner of that golf tournament was mentally stronger than all of the others in that one particular golf tournament. It does not take a rocket scientist to figure out why this is true. The following week it may well be someone else who wins a tournament, in fact more times than not, it will be someone different who was mentally stronger that week. The winners are for the most part those people who are more focused on their physical game

and on the golf course itself than all of the others who are playing in that same tournament, on the same course, putting the
same greens. Week after week another winner is crowned. In
1997 David Duval won three golf tournaments in a row. In the
year 2000 Tiger Woods, himself, won nine golf tournaments. Were
they so much better ball strikers than their opponents? Maybe
in those weeks they were, but be well assured that they were
confident about their games and about their skills. They were
more focused on their direction and their goals than their opponents were. They rode the horses until they fell off of them.

Many years ago Byron Nelson was an assistant pro at a golf
club in New Jersey where the Ryder Cup was being held. In
1935 he told some of his friends that one day he would be on
the Ryder Cup Team and they all laughed at him. Two years
later he was on that Ryder Cup Team. He was focused on his
goals. This is the same man who won 11 straight golf tournaments later in his career. I would imagine that his focus was ever
present in that run of victories, which may well never be equaled
by anyone.

Our focus and our mind-set make such a difference in everything we attempt to do merely because they make us better
at whatever we attempt to do, or they cause us to slide down
the slippery fire pole into those bitter pits of bad feelings and no
confidence about ourselves or our skills, as they relate to this
wonderful game. The reason this is a reality is easy to understand, at least for me, but so hard to remember when we lose
our focus and allow our minds to wander, like a homeless person trying to follow the warm sunshine. At that point the furthest
thing from our minds is focusing on anything relative to our golf
goals. That does not mean that we are not thinking about golf,
because we most likely are, but we are not focused on the task
at hand. We are mentally somewhere else. We might already be
on the next hole mentally roaming around thinking about what
is out there ahead for us. I have often stood over a short putt
and found myself thinking about something other than that putt.
I may be thinking about someone else in my life or some situation in my life and when I putt the ball it never even hits the

hole, let alone goes in the hole. My focus was not on that putt, but miles away. I probably could have handled whatever I was thinking about far better than I did the putt, which I missed so badly.

There are times when I say to myself that I am mentally strong enough to overcome all those flashes of non-brilliance, but I am more often wrong than right and the outcome will surely attest to that. I do know that when I feel this happening I should back away from the shot and come back more mentally focused, and therefore better equipped to make the putt or hit the shot.

Maybe we should stop here and think about what all of this means to us and how we need to approach this item of focus in the future. For a moment, consider just how we approach this game, which we all love so much. Because how we approach the game will determine how we play the game and to what extent our relationship with the game develops, mentally and physically.

Let's take for instance winning and losing. I have, on several occasions, heard the term "good loser," but I am not sure that anyone who is a good loser is or can be a winner. I would think that they might be too accustomed to losing, to be a winner. That doesn't mean that when we lose a match or a tournament we should act like a jackass or some kind of mindless idiot. I know that when I lose a match I am unhappy with myself merely because I did not play at my best. I am always ready to congratulate someone who beats me, but inside I am unhappy with myself. I am not angry with my opponent, because he did what I wanted to do. He won.

On the opposite side of the table there are winners who are not good winners. When a person is not a good winner, he or she is far worse than a bad loser will ever be. When a person wins at whatever he or she is doing and gloats and chortles about that victory, that is not only pretty difficult to take, from a loser's point of view, but it also shows that certain people have not been accustomed to winning often in the past. This sport is such a stately game it would seem that humility should have a place in it somewhere. All of that non-gamesmanship "gamesmanship" can easily be avoided and the whole affair will be far more pleasant and the memories will be far less tarnished.

I am sure that on a shelf, a table, or a bookcase somewhere in their home, most people who have played this game must have a trophy of some sort, be it small or grand, to remind them that they had a special day that they will remember for a long time in their golf life. No matter whether a person is a 0-handicap player or a 36-handicap player there has been a time in their golf journey that will forever have a positive place in their memory storage bin of joys. A time when they rose up or the competition fell down and that tray, trophy, or statue was theirs to keep forever, as a symbol of that special time of excellence in their golf life. I have been fortunate in my life, to have won a trophy or two. Still the best memories I have of this great game are not the results of trophies earned, except as they are represented by the imprints in my mind and on my heart of a place I played and special friends who made the package whole and wonderful and yes, priceless.

As I mentioned in a previous chapter, I have had two 62s in my life. One was well put together, with shots that could have only come in my wildest dreams and putts that I can only dream about making to this day. The other one was filled with shots that got only perfect bounces, hops, and skips. The results were the same, 62, but the trip to that number was entirely and vastly different. One was filled with work and a great deal of body English while the other was filled with good, smooth swings and mental ease. Though they both resulted in the bringing home of a trophy, I do not remember the trophies themselves. I do, on the other hand, remember the scores and the great joy I received from shooting them. Yes the trophies are there somewhere in my garage, but I do not need them to remind me of those two days in my golf life, where I was, what time of day it was, or whether it was cloudy or sunny. I do not need them to remind me that on at least two days in my golf life I was the best player in those neighborhoods. That is what golf can do for us, whether the score is 82 or 62.

I have heard people ask themselves time and time again, "Why do I play this stupid game?" I can only speak for myself and say that one of the many reasons I have to play this game is simply because I love the mental exercise it allows me, the inner self-contest the game causes to happen inside my head. It surely is not the only game in town, but for me it is the best game in town. Other people probably have their own reasons for playing golf, like it grants them peace; exercise when they walk 18 holes; they need to get away from work, wives, husbands. But all of those reasons for playing golf are only excuses for going out and playing the game. People play golf because they love it and they love the feeling of loving it. They love the emotions golf grants them. For some it is truly attached to their soul. Above all, the game of golf is not stupid. It only has the mentality that we give it. Think about that the next time you say, "I hate this stupid game."

Golf was for many years a game for only the wealthy. Today golf is enjoyed by people from every walk of life. You can go almost anywhere in the United States and find a golf course. Farmlands have golf courses and the farmers are now golfing. They have cowboy boots with golf cleats on them. The mountains have golf courses and the deserts are seeing golf courses being built by leaps and bounds.

To the average person, who looks at the growth of golf course construction in this country, it might seem that the people who build all of these golf courses are overbuilding. Yet there are people constantly playing golf on all of the new and old golf courses around this country. Many universities have their own golf courses and many intelligent people are playing this game, as well as people from the other side of that mentally elevated picture. The unemployed play golf. The one reason above all others that draws so many different people to this sport is that they love what it gives to them. They love the feeling levels they go through while playing this wonderful game. Even when it is bad, it is good. What else is like that?

It is obvious that some people are better at this game than others are, as in any sport. The reasons for this reality are numerous: talent, desire, practice, the right attitude (which includes patience), the correct equipment, and above all, the reason they had for starting to play golf in the beginning, whatever that reason might have been. What people get from the game and what they give to the game, are all reasons why some people are better than others at this game. What separates all of the great players from the rest of us is merely all of the above. What separates the single digit golfers from those who are not so fortunate to be single digit players, is merely some of the above. Two of those items mentioned above are patience and practice. The key to practice is to do so correctly, with the right movements, motions, and motivations—but above all doing it.

Taking all of the aforementioned elements into consideration, it is easy to see what golf can offer us. It offers us peace, pain, joy, sorrow and negativity, positiveness, companionship, solitude, challenge, hope, victory, defeat; but in the final analyze it offers us a true sense of victory. Above all else it offers us victory in more ways than just taking home the cup of victory.

Golf in reality does offer different people different things, according to their needs, their wishes, their skills, and their levels of risk taking. We can get so much from this game or we can get just a little bit of what it has to offer. All of that is up to the person holding the club, the amount of time he or she holds that club, and how they hold that club. Above all else, what matters most of all is why they hold the golf club.

Issac Newton figured out and stated, "Every object travels in a straight line unless it is acted upon by an outside force." If we simply remember this it will allow us to better understand a great deal about what happens in a golf swing and at impact with the golf ball. How we hold the club does make an incredible amount of difference in how the golf ball travels, straight or otherwise. The same is true in the total arc of the golf swing. This game of golf is a perfect example of the need for willpower. In order to find deep success in golf and the true and total benefits of participating in this game we need to have willpower. Weight watchers, both the individuals and the organization, are always talking about willpower. That is because to lose weight or to keep that weight off takes dedication, and to sustain dedication it takes willpower. To be able to accomplish most things in our lives it takes willpower.

Golf is no different. In order to stay on a path to perfection in this game of golf, it takes willpower. Of course perfection, as most people already know, seldom ever comes, but the carrot is always dangling out there ready to pull us forward toward that awesome goal. As you read these words and you are fortunate enough to be a 9-handicap-or-less golfer, you are in a small minority of golfers in the entire world. Maybe one-tenth of one percent. That is indeed a small minority.

Most of us got to where we are, not by accident. I say this because few people are blessed with skills that would allow them to be an above-average golfer and never practice. I know few, if any, who are natural enough at this game, to play it seldom and practice even less and still be above-average in their abilities. Some people are reputed to be naturals in many sports and that may well be the case, but in this most difficult of sports to perfect, if perfection is even possible, I doubt that there are many people who play golf who would fit into that category. Most of the great players whom we watch on television, week after week, seem to have such a fluidity in their golf swings. They do! They look good because they have worked at that swing for many years. It takes willpower to be good at anything, including life itself. Golf, though we sometimes may think that it is, is not greater than life. Therefore it will take willpower, on our part, to do all the things needed to make our emotional investment in this great game really pay off.

There are people who play this game in a special state of prominence, but they also have unbelievable work ethics, far above most of the people who own a set of golf clubs. Why? The answer is quite simple: they have the willpower to fit their needed work ethic and they understand why that work ethic and the work itself is needed. They practice for hours at a time. They have definite goals they have set for themselves. If I go out to practice and I hit two hundred and fifty balls in a practice session, some of my friends might say that it is great to have that kind of desire and that sort of drive and work ethic to practice so much. I know it means that I love this game and I want to work hard to be better at it.

Then I read how Greg Norman injured himself during a practice session that lasted six hours. Greg Norman, like so many others, is able to reach down inside himself and push those buttons that drive him to find the maximum amount of willpower to meet his specific goals. He, like many others in that business, is able to create more and more willpower to push him further and further along, to be better and far above those who crowd around him. Secretly that is what we all want, is it not, to be better than the crowd with which we associate? The better we get the smaller that crowd becomes and the closer we are to perfection. That is what players of all levels strive for, if they have a desire to be better. In order for that to begin to happen we first need willpower, which will force us emotionally to try harder and harder to get better and better. Practice will then have a reason for existence.

This game is best played when we are in our own little world. It is best played when we are safely inside of our own heads, for it is there that we can truly allow good things to happen to us and with our games. Take for instance one's golf game when they play alone. There are few outside distractions to fill up the mind. The scores and the shots show that they are better alone.

Many people try to get inside other people's heads instead of concentrating on what is going on inside of their own minds. Too much of trying to psych someone else out can often cause them (the psycher) to lose focus, and therefore the attempt to distract someone else has caused a distraction in the psycher's own game and game plan. A mind has indeed been tainted and compromised, but it is the mind of the psycher and not the psychee that has often been damaged.

The difference between winners and losers at any level of this game, depends on how deep and how long we can stay inside our own heads as we approach and play this game. Once we realize that this is our world and we feel truly comfortable in that ownership, then we will play better as well as differently, because we will work harder and differently in the pursuit of our game's true excellence. When a person feels this, he or she will be able, at that point, to define his goals and therefore understand the direction he needs to take to be better at this game. Everyone who plays or tries to play this game needs to be constantly aware that it is one thing to have a fire in your belly for this game and yet another thing to find a way to fuel that fire constantly, lest it goes out and the fire turns to cold ashes, becoming less than useful in our quest for perfection.

There is definitely a mind-body relationship, which needs to occur in each of us to succeed at this wonderful game. When and if we can tie the two of these issues together in some state of harmony, then and only then, can good things happen in a continual manner. Conversely bad things can occur in our game if there is no union of body and mind. This is not to say that good things will not happen if someone goes about their pursuit of perfection in golf in a haphazard fashion. The difference is that perfection for those who are haphazard and those who are not haphazard are totally different levels of pleasure and achievement and that in itself is all right. This game will continue to bring us joy no matter what level of dedication we might have in our relationship with it. That is the nature of the game itself, to bring us joy. In that respect, as well as others, I am sure life is basically the same as are the spiritual aspects of life. We can enjoy good and warm feelings from life even if we do not put a great deal of energy into making those feelings happen. Our spiritual life is the same. On the other hand each of these elements are a great deal better if they are pursued with dedication and respect for what they are.

Just take for instance the issue of swinging the golf club at a golf ball. If we do it from habit, that is not a sound approach to learning the true art of swinging a golf club or maintaining a solid and sufficient golf swing. We need to be ready mentally, as well as physically, to strike the golf ball correctly and in a repetitive manner. Repetition is vastly different from habit. As boring as repetition is, in many aspects of life, it is important in building and executing a sound and solid golf swing. Remember that a swing that begins with a mind-body relationship cannot be an habitual act.

It is so easy for someone to just go out and try to attack the golf ball when your mind is not yet ready to have that act occur. A good example of this is to observe the practice area, wherever you play your golf, before you go out for your next round of golf. Some people will inevitably come running to the practice tee and grab a range ball or two from friends or whomever might be in the practice area. They throw the golf balls down on the ground and swing hard and fast at them. If they mishit the practice ball they blame that bad shot on being in a hurry. But we all know they mishit the ball because they were not warmed up and the body was not ready to catch up with the mind. I am one of those people who feels cheated if I do not have time to warm up properly, before I play a round of golf.

First of all I miss just hitting golf balls and second, I will never play as well cold and unlimber as I will when I am sufficiently warmed up and loose, with all of my body parts feeling fluid and in sync. The older one gets the more warm-up time it takes to properly get limber and loose. Before I play any round of golf I feel an obligation to get to the golf course early enough to be able to warm up sufficiently and be ready when my turn comes to hit that first and fearful shot off of the 1st tee. Again getting there early enough to properly warm up takes willpower. That takes planning and it especially takes desire.

I call this PPPFF. Those letters always remind me that it takes Prior Planning to Prevent Future Failure. The responsibility in this situation is of course mine, to find a way, to get ready to play when my next round of golf happens. That should be woven in as part of the love we have for this game. I am sure that many people share this emotion with me. If we love golf so much, then why not do everything in our power to achieve the best possible results in our relationship with the game and in each round of golf we are fortunate enough to play.

When we allow our minds a chance to help us in any of life's pursuits many wonderful things can happen. This of course includes golf. There are two basic elements we have to beat in this game, on our way to perfection. They can truly be huge and strong adversaries as we work our way toward that often elusive level of perfection in golf. If these two elements are taken care of then we can possibly conquer the unconquerable. These opponents are the golf course on which we stand as we ready ourselves to play on any given day, and of course the other is our mind. The mind will try to play tricks on us and it often does, according to the latitude we give it. Just as each golf course has its spots of harshness, so the mind also has its areas where it is relentless, if it is allowed the freedom to wander and wonder.

Just playing against ourselves and the golf course will take a great deal of willpower and patience in order for us to win. Those golfers who fail to be able to control their minds will find themselves having some frustrating hours on the fairways, in the rough, and on the greens of the golf courses, wherever they play. That is part and parcel of what makes this game the greatest game going, merely because if we play it we cannot allow ourselves to let up mentally for one minute or the golf course will win and therefore eat our lunch—so to speak.

The best players in the world, on all of the tours and even in our home golf clubs, are the heady players. They are the people who can make something out of nothing, because they feel they can do just that. These people might miss a shot here and there, but they would not jeopardize their entire round of golf by being stupid and taking a chance on a shot they cannot make, merely because they do not have that particular shot in their repertoire or it might be an impossible shot to achieve. This might be different, if indeed that person was in a match play situation. The best players will, most of the time, try to put themselves back into a position to save par or at least give themselves a chance to make a run at par. These people would never reach into their golf bag for an old ball when approaching a hole with a water hazard or a deep ditch on it. To them that would be admitting they did not mind losing the old ball. That is in reality giving way to negativity. A smart player would think that he or she could hit that ball over the water or they might not even think about the water in the first place. They would probably think

202 • YOU WILL FIND A WAY

beyond the water, to the target, or even think about playing a shot that would take the hazard out of play.

When we begin thinking about whether we can hit a shot over a hazard then doubt, which of course is the dark visitor, has been admitted to the party and the player is no longer just playing against the golf course and himself—he is also playing against doubt. One has to think beyond the water, to the green and whether the ball will stop on the green or not. We need to find the peace that this game can bring to us and not allow ourselves to be burdened down and gobbled up by the negative issues that often can and do obsess us. The game of golf, as great as it is, does not need any help in being difficult. When we become absorbed by negative issues we become losers instead of winners.

Life is much the same way. It is human nature often to dwell on and lock into the negative sides of life and simply forget just how fortunate we are with all of the positive things most people have in their lives. Therein is yet another parallel with how we approach our relationship with golf. We will rant and rave about our bad bounces and hardly ever mention the good bounces, which happen in our golf lives quite often. It is true, that on many occasions, those good hops saved our scores from being even higher than they turned out to be. I doubt few people even think about that part of this mind-related aspect of golf. Now, that doubt, at least on my part, is acceptable here, but not beyond. We need help and not hindrance. Doubt about one's own ability is indeed a hindrance. If we have doubts about a certain part of our golf game then we need to get help with that flawed area, to try and fix whatever problem might exist.

It is easy many times to wallow around in self-pity with some sort of belief system that if something is broken and we cannot fix it, then we are weak or even more unrealistic, it will get secretly fixed by magic. Someone once said, be it true or false, "Therapists are for the wealthy and for the rest of us there is golf." The only problem with that theory is that golf can also make us needful of someone to talk to, because it brings many feelings to the surface when times are difficult. If you need help with our golf game, go and get it, but get it from someone who knows what they are talking about. Once you find that right person to help you, then you have to do your part and that part is you have to listen, be patient, and practice.

When we think and talk about the actual act of hitting a golf ball and the hard road that literally takes us to the place where we can safely assume we are going to hit the ball, when we attempt to do so, we have to take many of the things into consideration which have already been discussed. Things like lessons, learning about the many aspects of this game, practice, attitudes, emotions, peace, confidence, and oneself. Yet before we can fill our minds with all of these elements, which then tells our bodies how to react, we must decide just where our desire level is, relative to this game, and what we want and need golf to be for us. Do we want to play golf for social purposes? Are we interested in the exercise, mental and physical, that golf can afford us? Are we looking for a good walk on a beautiful day and the peace that can be ours for the asking and the taking? Are we about chasing goals and trophies? There are so many more questions that can be asked, depending on where we are in our journey.

Once those parameters are established, then maybe we will have a better idea as to the way we need to approach our pursuit of whatever our goals are in relationship to golf. If you need help, then get it. Remember also and foremost that lessons are good, at least good lessons are good. Remember too that this is your golf game and you should not pay to have it be painful for you or void of the happiness and joy this game can and will provide for you under certain circumstances.

For many years I held tightly to the theory that to play this game well a person had to understand the 2 Ds: Distance and Direction. It seems I might have been just a bit shortsighted, as it relates to those numbers and letters. Let me explain. In my early years of golf I considered my theory gospel. The truth of the matter is that a person who is strong enough to hit a 300-yard drive is not always the best player in town. Oh yes, he can hit the golf ball out of sight, but can he find it? Distance is helpful, but finding the ball once it is hit is often even a far greater prize. In order to achieve a wonderful level of golf efficiency it takes a great deal of dedication. In reality there are not just 2 Ds, there are 3 Ds—distance, direction, and dedication. The first of these 3 Ds, which enters most people's mind of course, is distance. That is what everyone craves and strives for. We do exercises to hit the ball farther and even higher. That, to the average person, is the element that separates great golfers from the humble and huddled masses.

Then there is direction. If someone hits the golf ball always or at least most always where he can find it, that is considered boring to many because maybe it is not as far down the fairway as the long ball strikers have hit their shots. Still strangely enough those players who are able to keep the ball constantly in play are the envy many times of those who have problems finding their golf balls, to hit their next shots. Hitting the golf ball straight is not a natural, skilled achievement. It comes about, if it is going to at all, because of knowledge and dedication. Many of the great professional golfers have in the past, or still do, hit their golf shots with fades or draws. They play those shots because that is how they achieve their direction; they train themselves to hit their targets with those types of shots. How someone hits a shot is not as important as successfully hitting that shot at the intended target.

There is also dedication. Dedication can just possibly allow the previous two elements to be introduced into one's golf games. Here are our 3 Ds. They are self-explanatory and logical in their concept and their place in our golf lives. It is important to remember that the best part of any theory, be it golf or life in general, is the action that follows that theory.

As I mentioned earlier in Chapter Fourteen, there are also 3 Ps to go along with the 3 Ds: Practice, Patience, and Perseverance. Both sets of these letters are of equal importance in learning more about and continuing to play this great game better and better. This game is a long journey if we are trying to reach perfection and we need every bit of help we can muster to play it at our best. The 3 Ps will help.

To be really happy with golf and to have fun at this game one needs to practice, and that means practice correctly and practice every aspect of the game of golf often and with reverence. A person should literally try to take his or her golf game to another level with each practice session. Those changes might be unnoticeable to most who observe a person's golf swing, but to each of us who knows our own golf game, we should constantly see and feel a difference. It is true that the better we get at this game, the smaller the improvements will become. We need to practice until and beyond the place and time where we feel positive and confident about our skill level. That means chipping, putting, all of the irons and woods (metals) and not just our favorite ones. Our level of confidence should grow with each session. Of course, as stated above, the amount of growth could be miniscule, yet it is growth and that should be our goal.

It takes a great deal of patience to play this game and play it well. There are thousands of people out there playing this game with a tremendous amount of skill and physical talent and little patience. Those people, at the first sign of a bad bounce or a negative break send clubs flying, and also words of negativity. They are quick to anger and quick to get down on themselves for their lack of talent and/or their bad fortune. They fail to realize that all of those bad breaks go along with all of the good breaks, to make golf just what it is for all of us. Patience allows rational thinking to surface and therefore it also allows survival to happen in a round of golf or in life itself. Patience is actually the element that brings about the proof of all of the theories we read about and/or come up with on our own—that is, if any of those theories are truly valid, or even provable outside of oneself.

Here is where perseverance either does or does not arrive on the scene. In Chapter Fourteen, I mentioned that these categories and the way we use them and line them up in our lives, will have a great deal to do with our success or failure in life and that often (maybe always) carries directly over into our golf. Without that third P in your lineup of letters you can literally kiss your accomplishing excellence in this game adios. This letter is what keeps people on the practice tee for hours at a time and on the putting green until their backs are sore from just bending over the putter. Perseverance keeps us working on faulty swings and putting strokes until those strokes are at least a bit better— not just better in our minds, but in our actual strokes and swings at the golf ball. This approach to the game of golf allows new days to break in our golf game and our handicaps to be lowered. This is another element that allows more enjoyment to creep into our games of golf.

There have been times, as I have alluded to in an earlier chapter, when this game has brought tears to my eyes just because of how humble I feel because of this game of golf. I guess that this level of emotion has often happened to me because I feel so blessed, to not only be playing this great game, but because of the peace of mind that this game offers me and this is not to mention all of the other elements which it has brought into my life. There have been times when I have been standing on a point somewhere overlooking a body of water, after putting out on a green and I have thought just how perfect that whole time seemed to be. There, at that moment, was little chance of stopping a tear of joy and/or sentiment, from rolling down my cheek. I recall reading part of the early portions of this book to some dear friends and as I mentioned earlier the tears came. Why? I guess because I love this game so much and I feel special things relative to the places it has taken me, physically, mentally and spiritually. I also believe part of that emotion comes from realizing just how this game has brought me together with special friends through the years and how it has literally joined us together in many aspects, as a family.

As I mentioned, some things in life are seemingly attached to our souls. Those things are often special to us because of their purity. So it is with this game of golf for me. It is pure and it is attached to my soul.

Hopefully, we will mature through the years in our relationship to golf, and that should be our desire. Most, if not all, who play this grand game want to move beyond just whacking the golf ball to striking it. We can find many treasures out there on our voyage to perfection, not the least of which is the peace golf can offer us, if we care to venture in that direction. There may be one or two or even more incidents in each person's golf life, as there have been in mine, that have given the game of golf its true purpose for them. In that time, there was most likely a signal or two of the things golf can and will afford them, if they are open to those events happening in their golf life. All of a sudden, after many swings and putts and trips to the driving range, the light may come on and a person may realize that this game of golf is something that is supposed to bring us joy and peace, not all of those negative feelings and emotions which have been experienced. It is a game of pluses, not minuses.

What matters most in this game are the good things that happen to us because of it, and not all of the things we consider to be bad breaks. A bad golf day is better than most good days of doing just about anything else. This game is about a relationship with ourselves, that inner place where moral and ethical decisions are made, and the joining of ourselves to a true positiveness with this sport. It is about a relationship with friends and their joys and sorrows. It is about a relationship with that spiritual other, which can give our whole existence a center, so peace can truly come into our lives and there abide in golf and life.

This game is more than a walk in the park, a swing at a little white ball, and the writing of numbers on a small card to denote the plus and minus side of the golf score. It is about mental and physical things. It is about spirituality and a closeness to nature and the creator of that nature. Golf is a complicated thing or it is simple. No matter how you approach it, it is a game to be played in joy and honor and in so doing we give it the just rewards of its high place in the total spectrum of games created by man for man. I feel it is an honor to play this game and to be able to sit here and write about it, feeling the way that I do about it. I feel it is a joy and an honor to sit and talk with my friends about the game of golf. That is true because of how I feel about them, both the friends and the game of golf. If I did not care for the people, I would not be sitting there talking to them about much of anything, important or not so important. On the other hand, if I did not feel the way I do about the wonderful world of golf, I would not talk to anyone about it or even play the game in the first place. I would urge each person who wants to really get to know this game, to go confidently in the direction of your dreams and do so with a joyous passion. In whatever you attempt to do, "you will never be defeated until you give up trying." Of course that includes golf.

Henry Beecher said it best many years ago and he was not talking about golf, but it fits nicely when we think about golf: "There can be no high civilization where there is not ample time for leisure." This game is a time to have leisure, no matter on what level your attachment to it might be. Enjoy your relationship with this gift that has been handed to you. We need to live all the days of our lives to the fullest and this game will afford us that quality of life, if we let it.

Some things in life are seemingly attached to our souls. Those things are special to us, as I stated previously, for many reasons. For me, more than any other reason, those things become close to me because of their purity. So it is with this game of golf. It is because of its purity that golf is attached to my soul!

> *To feel the fingers of touch from something that*
>   *fires your soul*
> *Is to be attuned to the source that molds your*
>   *emotional existence.*
> *To see the days come and go realizing that*
>   *memories are only fibers of life past,*
> *And once I stand and look out across this expanse,*
>   *my eyes will tell all I feel.*
> *No words need to fill the air, for kindred souls*
>   *have few secrets.*
> *If someone cares enough about me and I them, our*
>   *thoughts will be revealed.*
> *It is true that thoughts are only part of what*
>   *gives life,*

There is also sight and there are needs, all filled
with emotion and often crisis.
I must go to the garden again on the morrow, for
that fills a need in me.
In that place is warmth, joy, and fulfillment, all of
which this journey can birth.
I am no different than most, I have pain and I
know joy,
Both can be crucial to the firing up of my soul.
The things in my life, this grassy mound overlooking
the sea,
The friends who give my life true meaning and
love and never fear to show it,
All of the elements that have turned my life into
a joyous place to be,
I am so thankful for all of the reasons for the
firing up of my soul.

CHAPTER TWENTY

The Old Man and the Young Man (Decisions)

It was truly a rainy night in Georgia and the heat was promi-nent as the three young men sat cloistered together in a corner room, in the old Bon Air Hotel in Augusta. A rather heavy April thunderstorm was making it an easy night to stay inside of the old hotel and out of the pouring rain. These three young men, like literally thousands of other people, were nearly to the point of praying that the rain would subside and the great tourna-ment would be able to finish on the following day. All of these people had come to watch their heroes, in this great game, play for that coveted green jacket.

On this close and humid night the three boys, barely men, sat playing cards and feeling time slip by so slowly, as it seems always to do when one is bored and confined to only one place for what seems to be an eternity to young and energetic minds. Occasionally the thunder would strike and the lighting would light up the raindrops like prisms, as they bashed against the windowpanes, following the commandments of the bodacious wind. It was so warm in the Bon Air Hotel that night the boys

211

had to keep their door open to get some semblance of a breeze into their room. The would-be air conditioner, which was sitting in one of the windows, was failing miserably at its job, making it even more imperative that the door remain open. Each of the boys would take their turn dealing the cards and calling out their favorite card game to be played. Each would win and then lose and the cycle would, of course, repeat itself. The game was now in its second hour. The three—two students and a bank employee—were good friends. Though the friendship was young in age, it was not so in warmth.

After many hands of cards and a lot of laughter, the boys heard the ancient elevator creeping up from the floors below and they knew someone was coming up from the lobby of the old hotel. The sound of the old elevator was hard not to notice, with all of its scraping and grinding. They each turned and looked down the hallway of the hotel, as they did each time they heard the elevator doors open. This time the passenger was an older gentleman and he seemed to be just a bit under the weather, alcohol-wise. He turned right out of the elevator and stopped outside of the boy's door, looked inside of the room, and then drew a bit closer to the doorway. He was quite unsteady on his feet. "What in the hell are you boys doing?" the old man asked.

One of the three, in a joking manner, said to the older man, "We are playing poker. Why don't you come on in and get your money out and play a hand or two with us?" The older man seemed to be angered by the brashness of the younger man and informed the boys that he was going to his room and calling the front desk to get the security police up there to investigate just what was going on in their room. Of course they all laughed at the old man and he then disappeared down the hallway toward his own room.

It was not long before he once again appeared at the doorway of the boys' room. By this time he had removed his suit coat and striped tie. He inquired again, "What are you boys doing in here?" He sounded almost angry at this point and of course that prompted the boys to joke with him more and more. Then he slowly made his way into the room and sat down on the end of one of the beds. He pointed to one of the young men and asked, "What do you do?" He was told by the young man that he worked in one of the banks in Atlanta. "Which bank?" inquired the old man, and the younger man told him the bank for which he worked. The old man said, "That is where I keep all of my money."

"How much money do you have?" asked one of the boys. The older man sort of bobbed his head a bit and then informed the asker he did not know how much money he had. His words were, "I have someone who takes care of that kind of thing for me." He then turned to the other two boys and asked them what they did. One of the young men told him he was a student at Georgia Tech in Atlanta. The second of the two students told the old man he was a student at the seminary at Emory University. The older man then told the three that his grandfather had been a bishop in the Methodist Church. The young seminarian, full of morality and ethics but still too young in his approach to people, responded to the older man by saying, "Look at you now. Your grandfather would really be proud of you, if he could see you now." The old man looked hurt, got up from the corner of the bed, where he had been sitting, and left the room in a hurry. The young men looked at each other and did not know quite what to say or think about that weird encounter. At that moment the young seminarian was sorry for his brash comment.

It was not long before the old man was back again and this time he was undressed down to his sleeveless undershirt and pants. He had removed his shoes and there he stood in the door of the room in his socked feet. Then he walked on into the room once again, looked straight into the eyes of the seminary student, and asked, "Will you pray with me?" Of course, once the shock was over, the two of them did do just that. The old man fell asleep there on his knees, beside one of the beds, praying words that soon became indistinguishable to the two other young men who sat there watching all of this in astonished amazement. The three younger men literally picked up the old man, carried him down the hallway to his own room, and put him into his bed. The seminary student placed a short note beside the older man's bed that read, "I believe it was not just by coincidence that you happened to come by our room tonight. May God bless you. I am sure your grandfather would have been happy that you took the time to say your prayers tonight." Then he signed the note and the three left the old man to sleep off his night of drinking and praying.

As you read this you are probably thinking, "What in the world does this have to do with golf?" That is certainly an understandable question. The young man from the seminary and the older man became good friends through the next year or so. They spent time playing golf together and getting to know one another. In that two-year period of time the younger man had finished his work at the university and had moved back to North Carolina to follow the profession he had been training for in seminary. The older man, on the other hand, watched as his wife slowly died of cancer. When she finally passed away he telephoned his young friend and asked if he could come and be with him at her funeral service. It was as if they were family. Flying to see the old man, the younger man thought about all of things that had transpired since they first met in Augusta, those four years before.

They had indeed played a great deal of golf together. The younger man had watched, when they played golf, as the older man would look around at all of the natural things that surrounded the golf course and quite often acknowledged their beauty. The younger man could easily see there was something special in his older friend's relationship with golf. There was a great deal more in it for the older man than just swinging at the golf ball, which to be honest, he never did do well. The older man just simply enjoyed where he was and what he was doing. He once told his younger friend that, "The peace I get from being on the golf course is what keeps me going when everything else around me is closing in on me." This was still going through the younger man's mind as the plane touched down at the airport in Atlanta.

Driving the short distance in the Avis rental car, from the airport to the home of his friend, the young man wondered just how many of his deep emotional feelings about the game of golf (though they were still blooming) and those parts of it that make him truly whole, he had received from the old man. He knew that his older friend had little talent to play the game of golf, but a great deal of love for it. "It had to have come from somewhere," he thought as he drove along Morningside Drive. The following two days the two spent talking about the old man's wife and about golf and about many issues affecting the now small world of the older man. The young man felt sometimes as if he was sitting at the feet of a philosopher and it was really good to listen for a change. He remembered the occasions when the old man and he had been playing golf together and he would often notice that the old man was just sitting in the golf cart and listening, but not to him. That is what the young man was doing now, just listening. He was to find out that just listening and watching on the golf course and in life itself are indeed blessings all on their own. Another lesson learned in a book filled with more lessons than can be counted or even remembered.

After staying a few days there in Atlanta with his old friend, the younger man returned to his home in North Carolina. Very shortly thereafter he received a telephone call from his elderly friend. He just wanted to say thank you for their friendship and he told his younger friend that he wanted to do something for him. "Let me send you somewhere, to a place where you can learn more and more about this game of golf, which you and I love so much. Maybe you can learn more for both of us. It may be that one day you might want to follow golf as your profession, instead of the ministry." The younger man was so surprised at what he was hearing that he was nearly speechless. This was a dream come true. "Think on it and I will await your call. You will do what is right, I know that. The money is not a problem."

The next few days passed slowly, as they have a habit of doing when there are pressures on one's head and in one's heart about decisions that need to be made. There were long walks around the local golf course, day and night. There were times for the young minister to stop and think about his future and to just listen to all of the sounds around him, which are not always noticeable when one is trying to play golf and when golf is all that really seems to matter. This was a dream come true for anyone who has ever loved this game and wanted to get closer to its roots and the pure genesis of the game itself. There was prayer time, but more in the area of thanks than in the area of guidance. This was truly the first time the two great loves in the young man's life had come together at a crossroads. They had always so easily coexisted and now they were needing more than ever to comingle for sure or they would devastatingly collide. He was wondering if he had skills good enough to be a professional golfer and, for that matter, he was also wondering how he was going to be as a minister. He was far too young in his profession at that point to make an accurate assessment of his skills, relative to his work. Time would only tell, and as I write these lines now I guess the story has been told. He already knew by the end of the telephone call just what he had to do. The reason he did have that knowledge was because he knew where his heart was and where those feelings could possibly take him, sort of. Still he had no idea really where the years ahead would take him. He could never have dreamed that what you have read in these pages would happen to him in his lifetime—and he still has some time left, I hope.

When he called his friend back and told him he had been given a special gift the night the old man came into that hotel room in Augusta, he could hear the older man gently sobbing on the other end of the phone line. He knew that it had been a gift given to both of them, granted to them through the courtesy of golf. He told his older friend he had been offered a chance to fulfill a dream, but that he felt he would be less than honest to himself if he did not continue in the direction in which he had started. The old man's comment to him was, "I knew that you would make the right choice and you did."

As I sit here now, all of these years removed from that telephone call, I realize once again that the old man was truly a blessing in my life. He could have been viewed as a temptation by some. Even to the fifty-two-year-old man who stood there over the old man's grave, thirty years after that phone call, saying some final words, as only a few people gathered around the graveside to say goodbye to him. To the young man, his would-be financial benefactor was a would-be challenge to choices he needed to make. Just another challenge in a long line of challenges in and out of the game of life and the game of golf. He represented a chance for that young student to chase a dream and strangely enough that darn thing has not stopped rolling yet.

All of this entanglement of joy was offered to both, the young man and older man and it was just another gift of golf. Only one of so many, if we are open for them to come into our lives. The young man learned to look at the trees, the birds, and the wonderful rocks and their amazing formations—and not just at the golf balls. He learned to watch the sky and not just the clock. He learned to spend hours in leisure and not in stress. He learned to appreciate life, nature, his family, his friends, and of course his golf. He learned that golf and God can coexist in a world that often seems to be concerned with one or the other or maybe even neither. He learned that gifts for us are indeed out there, tangible or not, if we are able to just listen to the good breaks and let the bad ones go. He still finds all of those things a special joy today.

This story is a true story and it grants us a rare look at what transpired in the life of one man who literally found a magic bottle, rubbed it, and it produced a real life genie who could and did grant him a wish. The genie could have been a temptation or he could have been a messenger. Indeed this genie could have been both. In this life we have to find our miracles and our visitations wherever we can. The young man (me) could have taken either road, but I took the one that is far less traveled, out of reason and not just circumstance. What would have happened had I gone to the left instead of the right? No one knows and I have no idea myself, except I feel I would never have been through this special odyssey and lived through all of the wonderful hours and thrills that have come into my life, in the fashion that I have been blessed to live them and have them in my life. This game of golf could never be any more attached to my soul than it is right now, as I write these words. That would be impossible, I believe. Still I have been wrong before. Maybe there is more out there waiting for me and for all of us. I need to keep searching. We all need to keep on searching. Was my choice the right choice, now all of these years later? When the dust cleared over the matter, in my mind and heart, I felt I had no other choice but the one I made. Yes it was the correct choice.

We all have choices to make in our lives, both as young men (women) and older men (women). Both of the men in this story had choices to make. They both made them and they both cherished their choices. I indeed was that young man and I have lived that special dream. Golf granted me the chance, because of being in that hot hotel room in Augusta, Georgia, to chase a dream, to catch that dream, and to play this game. Was it a coincidence? I think not. Many times, when I stand somewhere near a lake or on a high hill overlooking a golf course and see rocks and trees in strange yet wonderful formations, I am reminded once again that there are special gifts in our lives that have texture, but no texture greater than the texture that attaches them to our hearts, minds, and yes even to our souls. Those connections go straight to our wellspring of joy. They can be physical, mental, spiritual, or emotional, or indeed they can be all of those elements rolled up into one creation. I am so happy that I made the choices I did so many years ago, to pursue many things, and one of those was this game called golf. I feel that way not because I have a great deal of talent for this game of golf, but rather because I have a great desire to be a part of what it is. I am indeed among all men, most richly blessed.

As I said before, I have never won any major golf championships, like so many people who try to write books about this great sport of golf. They have special history with golf and they have resumes but indeed so do I, though our histories and resumes may be different. My area of expertise relative to this game of golf is from the area I referred to earlier as *the part of the heart*. In that category I have few rivals because of the love I have for this game, and the love I have for life in general. I can say this with the greatest of confidence.

I have been on many mountain tops experiencing incredible highs because of the game of golf and the joys in my life. I have also been in a few valleys. Most of those I do not remember, merely because they are not important to me, when I recognize the mountain tops for what they are, what they mean to me, and what they have given to me. I have walked heart and heart around many golf courses with good, wonderful, passionate, and warm friends and I have done the same alone. Both are good, because of the passion I (we) pursue. I am truly glad that with a great deal of help, *I did find a way.*

Oh yes, I have climbed a mountain
I have seem the water and green grass far below
I have felt the fangs of disappointment,
But I have bathed in joy so many more times than
  in pain
Because in those valleys the grass is always green
And the sun reflects happily off of the faces of
  good and dear friends.

WOW! GOLF

— CONCLUSION —

We have talked a great deal about perfection in these pages. Many people have pontificated about the impossibility of ever finding perfection in the game of golf. That to me is shortsightedness on their part. It is also sad that those people who believe that finding perfection in the game of golf is impossible, feel the way they do. As simply as I can state it, if we have a relationship with this game and it grants us peace and true joy, then we have attained a level of perfection that few can understand and yet many really can enjoy. What is the secret? There is no secret, except finding pleasure in something developed, through the years, solely for that purpose. We can be just what we are and who we are with our golf games or we can climb up that special skill ladder to being better at this game than we could have ever imagined. No matter where you and I are on this pole of talent, we can still be happy with this game, because after all is said and done that is indeed all that it is. A game. Enjoy it and find someone to enjoy it with. Look around you and take notice that these are beautiful gifts we have been given, this life we have and this game of golf. Golf shows us and others who we are inside and what we are made of. It shows our strengths and our weaknesses. It is a reflection of life itself—and remember, both golf and life are to be enjoyed.

This game should be a game of peace and it should take us to a place of peace. That peaceful place in our hearts and minds where golf is wonderfully intertwined is indeed "the Garden." It is in that place of peace where golf can become what it really was meant to be for each of us. Not many people find that spot, but those who do will never relinquish that special place in their hearts and minds to any other thing. Of course there is always room in "the Garden" for many more special feelings and special things.

This game is one you cannot win, unless victory in it comes from the love you have in your heart for the game, for the purity of the game, the peace that is in your mind just because you play the game, and the joy you have in your life because you have played and been a part of the greatest of games. I hope that golf and life are as good to you as they have been to me. If so you will be among all men (women), most richly blessed. Wow!

If you venture into "the Garden"
Be aware of your transgressions
Because they will be readily evident.
But on the other hand
If you truly walk in "the Garden" with a pure heart
And witness the pure, simple beauty of this game,
It will be a journey
Filled with so much joy and warmth
That you will never be able to remember it all.
And in "the Garden" there is peace.

I HOPE THERE IS NO END!

Give the Gift of

You Will Find a Way
to Your Friends and Colleagues

CHECK YOUR LEADING BOOKSTORE OR ORDER HERE

❏ **YES**, I want _____ copies of *You Will Find a Way* at $22.00 each, plus $4.95 shipping per book (California residents please add $1.60 sales tax per book). Canadian orders must be accompanied by a postal money order in U.S. funds. Allow 15 days for delivery.

❏ **YES**, I am interested in having Corbin L. Cherry speak or give a seminar to my company, association, school, or organization. Please send information.

My check or money order for $_____ is enclosed.

Name _____

Organization _____

Address _____

City/State/Zip _____

Phone_____ E-mail _____

Please make your check payable and return to:

HGG Publishers
245 Morningsun Ave.
Mill Valley, CA 94941